Tempus ORAL HISTORY *Series*

Byker
voices

Molineux Street back lane on 13 January 1914, with prominent advertisements for Beavens Furniture Store. Frederick Beaven employed many Byker girls. The photographer is standing in Shields Road and looking towards the North View end and the North Eastern Railway. (NCL)

Tempus ORAL HISTORY *Series*

Byker
voices

Compiled by
Ken Groundwater

TEMPUS

Tempus Publishing Limited
The Mill, Brimscombe Port,
Stroud, Gloucestershire, GL5 2QG

ISBN 0 7524 2201 4

Typesetting and origination by
Tempus Publishing Limited
Printed in Great Britain by
Midway Colour Print, Wiltshire

A scene from October 1897 of work going on at the Byker destructor sheds and furnaces. These were sited almost opposite Brough Park Stadium on the Fossway. (NCL)

Contents

Acknowledgements

My acknowledgements and thanks go to the editorial teams of the worthy *Byker Phoenix*. Although now defunct (or possibly just sleeping?) the *Phoenix* became not only a clearing-house for 'thinking' Byker but helped consolidate and make sense of all Byker had been through in the painful process of all that the word 'redevelopment' means. It also illustrated how Byker folk could continue to mock themselves in an enviable way reflecting there unique 'specialness' that it was my great fortune to experience. I've included some snippets and can only apologize for being unable to include more due to space limitations.

My family, and my extended 'Byker family', have admittedly underpinned my sources but I would also like to thank the matrons and staff at Lawrence Court on Allendale Road for allowing me to speak with residents. The *Evening Chronicle* kindly obliged by allowing me contact with some Byker contributors who, in turn, have consented to quotations from their source notes to facts that would otherwise been lost from memory.

Sirkka-Liisa Konttinen, the 'Byker Photographer' during the transition period, offered photographs and memories. The least I can do in return is to mention her website and encourage readers to visit Amber/Side at: www.amber-online.com.

I would also like to thank Keith Armstrong for some inspirational thoughts and Dave Bolland for his – all via the *Phoenix*! Also Jack Routledge who first sang 'Old Byker Bank' way back in 1967 at the Bay Hotel at Cullercoats, the lyrics of which have haunted me (and possibly many others) ever since. The excellent librarians at Newcastle City Library Local Studies section have, as usual, made research almost enjoyable.

I am grateful too to Ron French, who is simply the most knowledgeable person I know, and also to Mike Greatbatch, who helped inaugurate the Ouseburn Partnership project and has consequently done so much to encourage greater knowledge of this fascinating part of Newcastle. 0000My family have also put up with my anti-social behaviour towards them when I'm always 'nearly finished.'

Finally I would like to express my thanks to two special school pals who helped suffer the red-brick institution with me. They were both St Peter's Road lads: Billy Thompson and Douglas Stoddart. Sadly, I can no longer thank Doug in person. On that note it is always of some regret that the majority of people in the family photographs are not around to enjoy their past – albeit a hard past. The last of the older generation illustrated within, Charles Harrison, died whilst the book was in preparation, in August 2000, and worthy of an old Byker boy he had achieved the excellent score of ninety-one.

Some of the pictures are drawn from the collections of Newcastle City Library and from Evening Chronicle Newspapers Ltd, and I am grateful for permission to reproduce them here. They are denoted by the abbreviations NCL and EC respectively.

Introduction

Praise them that will times past, I joy to see
My self now lives: this age best pleaseth me
Robert Herrick

As a part of greater Newcastle, the name Byker has always been synonymous with the type of music-hall joke associated with a local humorist, 'the Little Waster' – Bobby Thompson. It has been mercilessly depicted as the *enfant terrible* of greater Tyneside and, with its close-knit reputation for street fighting, had difficulty casting off a perceived 'no-man's-land' status; that is until the advent of the renowned Byker Wall in the 1970s. The final 'blessing' to complete integration back into social acceptance came via the media when a local TV Company sold *Byker Grove* nationwide and suddenly Byker had been 'spun' as fashionable!

The housing grew out of green fields from 1875 with the urgent need to supply workers for heavy industries that were to take a grip on lives for four generations of Byker families. It grew in a haphazard sort of way, and some streets were built, as they were to end, in stumps here and there around gaps. But it was the community warmth that was to eventually be the epitaph of 'old Byker' when the houses fell. The generous nature of its people was the dominant memory, not unlike other tight industrial communities, where self-help, in its many forms, was an easily found natural commodity and social workers dared not intervene. The aged were gently respected and very visible – unlike today's disintegrated communities.

Yes it was grey-coated and its two parks were poorly equipped but there were spin-offs that fed the imaginative senses in the same way that the Brontës survived their own austere existence. The sights and sounds presented to the Byker child were powerful enough to last for more than one lifetime; and, talking of sounds, there were many. There were sounds that represented an order within the chaos and gave you a notion of the time of day or night. There were the cries of Saturday night's *Football Pink* lads for those eager to hear their 'pools' fate. There was the thump-thumping sound of a band practising somewhere that briefly came and went on the smoky wind as if controlled by a huge volume switch; there were Sunday morning's rude awakenings by the Boys' Brigade in full cry storming St Peter's Road (and taking no prisoners), but most of all there were factory buzzers that declared publicly 'You are workers, and are called to your work Mecca'. One in particular used for this job was an old air-raid siren.

There were more haphazard sounds associated with two sources that never stopped, and which sandwiched the community: the railway and the river. The low organ moan from the swing bridge would demand the response of a vessel in a world-weary way that echoed our sleeplessness. The steam whistle reply was about the foreign places we dreamt of as we spun semi-comatose on the roundabout in Harbottle Park, keeping our eye on sliding mast-tops in the river below. Or as we lay in bed awaiting the reply note, then hearing it, we turned over and slept and dreamt of Newcastle winning the cup again.

Readers who don't know this area will find Byker full of contradictory statements in the passages within and may feel no closer to understanding this strange place. It had everything, it had nothing. It was rich yet poor. Good yet bad. Ugly but in a beautiful way – as you may find when looking through the views. How can this be? I don't pretend to know, but simply present the facts through dialogue by the people, as evidence to support at least the theory that Byker was different, and still is!

The *new* Byker was made possible through close co-operation of a sort never known elsewhere at that time. It showed the degree of respect held for its people by a council who also acknowledged that just bulldozing would have seen riots and maybe worse. The council acted against the norm which was then to the effect that working-class aspirations stopped at an inside toilet. It seems fair to say that Byker folk recognize and honour loyalty above many other currently popular values and, eventually, allowed Erskine's dream to happen. They believed in him. They also, like bad children, can be fickle, and the wall dwellings were at once the worst and the best!

I feel my own personal memories of Byker can be no better summarised than from this description of a journey home one night on the No. 12 bus:

'I've waited for ten minutes in New Bridge Street in winter rain and cursed, along with more senior and drunk companions, the "three-come-at-once" theory. It comes. I'm downstairs in the bus and we all steam in our wet smoky conviviality in a hazy soup of togetherness. I notice among the "be-macked" travellers a family at the front with children. Late for them, I think. One lassie has a machine-gun-like violin case. The more drunk around me take longer to see this and I watch amusedly as I see their lights switch on and one by one their focus adjusts and their heads roll less. I wait and enjoy this wait, as you would those moments in time before something excellent occurs – similar, but different, to the anticipation of a penalty taken by Super Mac. It happens: a drunk shouts out, "Howay bonny lass, gis a tune!" The family need not be asked twice and are clearly deeply proud of their protégée. The lassie flushes and says, "Should I, Mam?"

'The entire downstairs bellows consent instead and the case opens to reveal a dark brown gloss that seems to match everyone's wishes. She plays, but is soon interrupted by drunks in various degrees of self-pity and remorse as they each croon in a different key accompanying her tune that resembles a caged bird's song in this unlikely setting – and we have an instant club.

'The conductor breaks into song and bizarrely interrupts himself with "Byker Bank", but for which signal, we would have forgotten this isn't a concert bus-trip but the Byker bus. The driver's jacket swings on his chair-back to the music. We are now clapping and a large woman attempts to dance in the aisle but is thrown back onto her seat as we turn down into Brinkburn Road. The lassie's mammy says we can have one more, "hinnies", and the oldest reveller, with a surfeit of liver marks, orders *Delilah*. Everyone takes it up before the violinist has bow to strings and I wonder why these unplanned "dos" are always the more memorable. As we near Commercial Road she makes a sudden bow. All our hearts are lost to childhood's sweet innocence. Her parents' pride reaching bursting point, they are manhandled down the aisle as silver reins upon the lassie and, "Tell her to stick in!" and "Ee, hin, that wes smashing!" go with them into the black night. The entire session has lasted but twenty minutes and we are reluctant to further dispel the magic and go past our stops. Reflecting on our bus party and the time I've just had, I'm awash with nostalgia, and eventually sleep in a perfect purple haze with the distant lights of Felling twinkling across the Tyne Gorge.'

CHAPTER 1
Childhood and Schooldays

Shields Road Woolworth's store, much beloved of small children, September 1955. (NCL)

First TV

My Auntie May was one of the first in our street to get TV but we all called it 'Tyne-Tees', never TV. One of the delights for us kids was seeing the many cartoons. I used to get into Auntie May's house when I knew *Popeye* was on around about tea-time. They would both get about silently washing up their brown cutlery as if I didn't exist whilst I would roll about laughing. I wasn't allowed to touch any TV controls – that again was adult domain and was certainly never tolerated in another's home. Sometimes they had the TV so quiet I would be almost on top of it but no one noticed and you would struggle on but durstn't mention you couldn't hear. That was how respectful the relationships were then.

May McClen

Anothe view of Shields Road Woolworth's store.

Playing Outdoors

We would play out from after breakfast the whole day long without any fear. We would just move from street game to street game. Footie 'doors' would last the longest time but other games were mounty-kitty, hide and seek, cricket with dustbin stops, running marathons... but mounty-kitty was the best. It was 'cause it got the less delicate girls brought into the games action and this was a chance to get ya hands on – if you know what I mean! We would have to bend and hold onto the person in front whilst someone had to leap over all the bottoms to reach the wall end without the bridge collapsing. It was great fun and really brought everyone and even the little 'uns out for a turn, and got them into playing with us big 'uns. It was the one game that got all the street together, which was quite unique really. We always made it boy, girl, boy etc. and when you became about eight or nine or so, these girl/boy games seemed to temporarily kick footie and cricket into touch – but not for long, we soon be back challenging the next street.

Stephen Maine

Street Fights

There were always gauntlets being thrown down for such and such to fight it out 'once and for all'. There were always formidable fighters in Byker and those who nonchalantly picked a fight with an unknown quantity could well regret it for quite a long time. This happened to a lad who lived next to Mickey Matfen in Ayton Road. He was unfortunately a bit on the simple side and ran into and picked a fight with someone from the East End Boxing Club. Now anyone else would have looked at his squashed nose and heavy, badly fitting eyelids and thought discretion was the better alternative. Alas, and too late, he found himself dumped by the roadside and in need of hospital care. He wasn't too hot to begin with but was thereafter unemployable and spent his remaining days on the dole and getting taken for a ride by many who didn't know him. The lads that did know him sort of looked after him and bought him the occasional pint but he was never the same again.

You tended to quickly develop a sixth sense when a trap was about. I remember walking down past Cheviot View towards the high wall that then surrounded St Michael's church when I got this smell of blood in my nostrils. It meant that there were Carricks or Malias about.

Ken Groundwater

Getting into Scrapes

We weren't always so goodie-goodie though. Byker had its mean streets where boarders were taken in and there was a certain amount of tension in the air. We knew roughly the area where shift-workers would be wanting to get to sleep and would clatter the windows with dirt and pebbles to get some action. It was the old battle-axes that we were most scared of as we thought they were more witch-like and rumours went around that Mrs

An unidentified but typical Byker back lane in Victorian times. The washing lines criss-cross down the lane; the coal man was the scourge of the washer-wives.

Adjacent to 206 Ayton Street, the author (right) celebrates his seventh birthday in fine back-lane style disguised as his favourite cowboy, The Lone Ranger. With him are 'best pals' Billy Thompson (left) and Douglas Stoddart. (It saddens me to relate that Doug lost his life in a road accident at the young age of twenty-eight years.)

So-and-so was able to cast spells. That was all it needed and we never went anyways near again. One evening, a gang of us decided to explore the back of the Co-op shops up on Allendale Road. We found all this food and decided to throw it around for the all the homeless cats and dogs that then constantly roamed the streets. It wasn't long before something like animal mass hysteria took over in the back lane from where we were chucking the food. The smell of the bacon rinds must have been the main trigger. What we hadn't reckoned on was anyone appearing out of the Co-op back door. Well, we were well trapped, weren't 'us! We couldn't get past the scrapping animals on one side and the approaching Co-op official. We were lucky to be let off but had to clean up all this fat and suchlike off the lane. The smell of our mitts was a problem when we got back yerm [home]!

Dick Potts

Unexpected Kindness

Occasionally us kids used to find a touch of kindness in the most unexpected places. I will always remember small incidents like the dustbin man that offered me a nearly new toy that some rich kid had thrown out. Then there was the ticket 'griper' that lived in a tiny pokey 'box' on the Heaton Road entrance to Heaton station. He somehow spared some time explaining to me – me, a filthy black snotty nine-year-old crow-kid – where a loco I had just seen could be located in my spotters' book. Such oases of kindliness were never forgotten and were clung to- proven by the fact that I still recall this today.

Ken Groundwater

Aback of the Co-op

These places aback of the Co-op shops got us all into trouble a few times because of the privacy they offered whilst we got up to some mischief. On one occasion we collected up there with two of the less delicate girls. There were four lads. We were only about six to seven. We started off trying on a few experimental things, like looking in each mouths, that sort of stuff. This progressed to touching tongues and it was just as well we were disturbed about then as it was progressing in a very dangerous way! We certainly knew what we were doing was wrong and ran till we reached home non-stop certain that the police would be calling to see our dads about us. God forbid this was tame to what the kids do today, but we were more easily shamed and lived in mortal fear of the 'pollis'.

Dick Potts

Inviting Girls Home

There was less intermixing between boys and girls then but I can't think why this was so. It certainly wasn't done to blatantly have a girlfriend before you were about sixteen, at the very least. I remember once I pestered me mam to invite this girl I liked back because me mam knew hers. I think it was Joan Allcock; anyway, her family came around to tea just so's I could have a bit of quiet time with Joan. Well after tea I went out with her to play but was spotted by my regular mates and in a panic I told Joan we were now playing fast running. I took her around the block so many times at full speed to avoid been caught by me mates that Joan was exhausted and naturally didn't think

Looking up Ayton Street with the Bolam Street schools at the top, c. 1966.

much of this game. She never again came to tea. I was about seven!

Stephen Maine

First Day at School

I remember my first day at Bolam Street Infants' School. For once I could get inside past those black, forbidding spiked railings and past the huge prison-like gates within which was the equally formidable redbrick barrier with little cube windows. I was keen to find out about all that went on behind this façade.

The first teacher I can remember was Miss Tulip. I think she looked ancient to me even then but I heard she went on to live into her eighties and died around the late 1980s. They had a tough time, these reception teachers. They had to be mothers to some of the kids. I can recall some mothers hanging around the gates long after we'd gone in, making the kids uncomfortable. They were hanging on all right. We were little animals out of the urban jungle – talk about rugrats, we were jungle rats. There were the normal early days' disasters taking place. Crying, peeing, accidents of the other kind galore and everyone asking when it was 'mammy-time' – but the incident I remember best was Brian Davidson's trousers being permanently stuck to him with the associated colourful smell that kids love to smell on others and point out with relish. When I look at the class group photo the smell is still almost tangible with his posture – most unkind, but there it is. It is fixed forever and cannot be deleted. First impressions are strong but none will ever again be like those associated with our first big unaccompanied steps into an unknown land.

Ken Groundwater

School Assembly

The awkward assembly: what to do with hands and feet? The white and delicate looking girl who was sickly and was the first one to keel over and was caught by her friend Jennifer – her with the bobbly thick hand-knit jumpers of many colours. Miss Tulip on the piano and those hymns classed as suitable for infants that went on and on and were more suitable for wakes. In the morning it would be 'Daisies are our si-ilver, Buttercups our gold; These are all the treasures we can have or hold.' Environmental lessons so soon!

Ken Groundwater

Games

The games we played were many. There was 'doors' and 'hot-rice' and too many others to recount. Those two I've mentioned and most others took such a toll out of shoe

A Harrison, McClen and Groundwater family get-away from Byker in 1954. They have surfaced here in the hills of Slaley. From left to right: Alex Groundwater, -?-, Moyra Harrison, Ivy Harrison, Charles Harrison, May McClen, Violet Groundwater and Joe McClen.

leather [still rationed at this time] that holes in the soles were just patched up with whatever came to hand, such as corn-flake packets.

We seldom needed to leave Byker, we didn't need to. A favourite haunt was the quayside. I well remember flying model aircraft from the banks near the old Velvet City area overlooking Spillers. Then there were the cigarettes picked up from visiting foreign sailors, Americans mostly then, and the grain dropped from trucks all around the granaries which we picked up and sold to the pigeon fanciers.

I remember a grate in front of Spillers which could be raised, even by us little kids,

Bolam Street School sports field, off Clifford Road, was where Newcastle jazz bands showed their talents at regattas and exhibition sports days. Harbottle Park is below.

and we'd lower a jam-jar or bottle tied to a piece of string. Upon re-emergence it was full to the brim with nice black sticky molasses – delicious! Pleasure then was simple and very cheap! Sometimes our well-worn pullovers bulged with oranges, grabbed as they fell from crates whilst being unloaded by the cranes on the quay. It was all just such a great huge adventure playground!

John Bonner

Daydreaming

We swung on our knees and looked aimlessly into Ayton Street beyond and as we sang we wondered what the 'mammies' would be doing without us and longed to be in those free streets. We hoped at first to get a glimpse of the mammies going about their business but never did and all too quickly shut that thought out as a step towards becoming conditioned and resigned to our imprisoned fate behind the little square windows containing cheerless half dead plants – the same plants that had so long fascinated us as outsiders!

The bits *between* assemblies were, for us boys in particular, mostly purgatory. We were often tired silly through the boredom of lacing coloured thread through bits of cardboard or repeatedly going over and over the same sentences of *Janet & John*. We were also hungry most times. This is when we began to develop daydreaming into a fine art that would be one of the most useful items we matriculated with and would stand us in good stead for the rest of our lives. We got to stare out of the square windows a lot and to dream. We could forget the worst – the hunger – the boredom and go off elsewhere, anywhere! We could be entertained for whole lessons by the drips forming on rainy panes and betting against an imaginary challenger upon how they would run. Anything external to do with this bleak austere classroom was where we longed to be. The fly outside – how lucky he was, but does he understand the real value of his freedom right now? You began virtual betting with anything that could move and so developed a habit of a lifetime that would lead us all to the door of 'honest Davie Kindness' and today Ladbrokes.

Ken Groundwater

The Headmistress

Things got steadily worse and one dank Monday – to add insult to injury – the headmistress announced that from this day, first lesson, would be especially for mental arithmetic tests, fresh from assembly. She was a mate for Scrooge. She was thin, wore exclusively black, and was pointed with manly spectacles and very little humour and she was now to greet us for a first double lesson to kick off the week with a bang!

If it was possible to add any more misery to our now nervy lives then she found it by choosing the location for her savagery as the unoccupied basement class that had no view because it was below pavement level. We could now clearly imagine being slaves in a galley.

The scene was set to ensure that we all learnt to fear and hate 'sums' in any form forever! In later life, when working with your own children, you come to learn that 'sums' are not so bad after all and you

The author surveys the mysterious world of Bolam Street School through those invidious barriers, 1952.

momentarily think to yourself that you may have been short-changed as a child and did our school days have to be quite so much a military operation. Mental arithmetic was an example of a forced-feeding technique. The Head had to ensure it was learnt or, it was considered you were a no-hoper thereafter. To be benevolent to her she did at least ensure that in a mere ten more years we would flood out the door and could assess if our expected meagre wages were about correct if not right on.

Ken Groundwater

Sun Ray Clinic

I remember they said the Sun Ray Clinic was one of the first ever when it opened up in the 1930s. This was before anyone had heard of such things then. We were curious but would rather not get involved because it meant you weren't very well if they sent you down there. It was situated in the old clinic in Brinkburn Street. I think it was the brainchild of Sir James Spence who I seem to remember opened the clinic. He was right and many folks said he was barmy when it first opened. Before long, loads of me mates were being sent there for this 'sun' treatment for all kinds of complaints but mainly for TB and rickets and things like that and most of them seemed to quite enjoy it. I think they had to don goggles and sit down in front of a lamp but it seemed to work. Everybody can't get enough of the sun today so maybe it was this lamp that put the thoughts there!

George Scott

Pocket Money

Memories of hot summer days include calling into to Mark Toney's ice cream parlour on Shields Road or buying a cornet from 'Julian' who, with his gammy leg, would journey all around Byker with his motor-cycle-driven cart. Byker was bustling with characters then. I remember the deaf and dumb man selling sticks from an old pram. Or the fish-seller with the fresh herring on a hand-cart, serving it baked in vinegar. All just memories now.

To get pocket money kids would buy cheese barrels from the L&N food warehouse off Brinkburn Street, chop them up and sell them as bundles of sticks for a penny. Rabbits were sold – in their skins mind – and, together with bundles of rags and jam-jars, were loaded onto bogies and sold at Freddie Shepherd's on Byker Bank. Rabbit-skins got 3d, 2lb jars one old penny.

John Bonner

Tough Girls

I can recall in winter the image of a duffel-coated mob – not unlike a many-footed and cloaked dervish that hurtled spinning, rushing, screaming, around the bleak frosted tarmac space engulfing anything that was caught up in its wake, and woe betide the girl that got swept up in the maelstrom. There were some, of course, who desired boy attention, but they were a nuisance and the things for amusement *after* the battle. Some girls gave as good as they got in the mêlée. These were nearly always from a big family and treat all boys as younger snotty-nosed brothers, you had to watch these amazons, they would think nothing of kicking you very hard.

Ken Groundwater

St Peter's Board School

St Peter's Board School opened July 1876 but met its centenary party as a closed, cold ruin as the bulldozers went in and the axe fell. Established in the Velvet City, it was typical of buildings close to the river mirk and was itself begrimed in years of industrial fallout. Tom Heslop describes how it was as a pupil there in the last years of the nineteenth century. His words were recorded in 1976 and are reproduced here courtesy of Joan Jemison.

The headmaster was Tommy Curry. He would wield his belt with the greatest dexterity if you drifted off. In conducting morning prayers he would have his 'victims' lined up in rows and they became paler as the prayers drew to a close. Provided I wasn't one of them I would look forward, in a pathetic way really when you think now, to the entertainment as Mr Curry got his belt and walloped over his desk those who had played the wag. I remember once I went to school this day by way of the Central Station – just three extra miles onto me journey! I wanted to see the men arriving home from the Boar War. It was July 1902. They marched briskly out the station and up to Fenham Barracks wearing khaki uniforms and I believe it was the first time we'd seen khaki in use. I was lucky because Mr Curry turned a blind eye on this occasion but I was warned.

We had to pay for schooling when I started. It was about 6d a week which was a lot. Some of me pals couldn't get in, and in addition didn't even have shoes. The Velvet City, as we called it, was a warm place then. We kids had a good time really, shoes or not! I remember on Shrove Tuesday, there was a parade of children carrying their pots down to the Velvet City where they eventually all went into the Fell Street Mission and sat on the floor to eat pancakes and drink tea, served and made for them by the ladies of St Lawrence's church. There was always quite a bit competition between us at St Peter's and those at St Anthony's School. We'd try and beat them at everything from handwriting contests to running. My grandfather was an engineer for the old Tyne Ferry Company. They went on strike in about 1818 and when it was over a stone to commemorate the event was eventually incorporated in a new building. The stone can still be seen above Timpson's shoe shop on Shields Road. Byker Bridge was also built around this time by C. Harrington. It was built privately and Harrington asked the council to buy it off him but they refused his price. So he simply blocked it off at both ends and introduced tolls. The council thought to beat him by routing folks another way across the Ouseburn but people liked his bridge and happily paid up. After a couple of years the council themselves knew they were beaten and had to cough up, only now Harrington charged them an extra couple of thousand for the delay.

Tom Heslop

One corner-shop of renown was Lydia's, on Bolam Street. It is seen here on a wet day in 1969.

A Bolam Street School class photograph dating from 1915. The class teacher is said to be Miss Phyllis and the only identified pupil so far is at the bottom right corner in the shape of William Henry Wallace. His son, Alan, subsequently became a Newcastle librarian and donated this photo to the library collection. (NCL)

Early Reader

Few people had books. I loved comics when they started to get better known in the early thirties. The library down near the egg factory became a great attraction when we could read a bit. Education was important now and we were encouraged, more than our fathers were, to go to the library. The librarian tested us; I think she was a Mrs Fairbrother. We were still so small we had to climb up onto a special high chair to see books that were only a short distance up the shelves. We were only allowed one at a time at first. It was a great honour when she allowed us two and then three etc. You felt bigger and cleverer than those still on one or two books.

This is how it happened. We got a reading test when we first went. She would say, 'Can you read this page?' I struggled to say the least at first and she said, 'Robert, you will have to tell your mam to teach you some harder words.' So off I went home and telt me ma and she did teach me a bit, but she was busy and said to practise on the food packets. So I did. The next time I went, she said again, 'Robert, can you read this?' and I sort of hoped it was the same page but she'd changed it and I messed it up, thinking it might be the same. I failed again. Anyway, I kept going and eventually I got through on about the sixth attempt and felt well pleased as I was still quite a poor reader but I so much wanted to join this club, you know. So she says: 'OK, but you can only have one book, you understand, and you can start with this same one.' Of course, what happened next was that I raced home, over the moon, and tells me ma that the lady says I'm a reader. She was more surprised than me and didn't at first believe me, so I produced my first book and she had to believe me, didn't she!

Anyway, I was quickly going through the books (or really the pictures) at one a day that the poor librarian got so sick of seeing me come and go that she let me have two books a day and I really thought I must be smart, and not even five years old. My mother used to repeat this story back to me so much out of pride that it must be one of my first memories of mesel'. It's a terrible thing, is a thirst for knowledge.

Robbie Harle

Rat Boy

The 'Rat Boy' made the national news quite frequently between 1989 and 1993. He became quite a character and earned media fame by disappearing into the central heating ducts in the Byker Wall development. He made up makeshift 'lairs' that his nine-year-old frame accessed easily but anyone larger had quite a bit of difficulty detecting. He was committing hundreds of minor (and some not so minor) offences and hiding away into his metal and concrete

A very relaxed family group congregate for Robbie Harle's (foreground) birthday in the hot summer of 1938 near Dilston Water, far from Byker's smog.

The Wall begins to loom over Raby Street back lanes, 1973.

Empire Day

Another cause for celebration was Empire Day when we got a half day off school. We would march into school and wore a uniform representing each of the organizations, i.e. Brownies, Scouts, Red Cross etc. Weeks were spent practising for this auspicious display which was sometimes, in front of civic dignitaries. We would sing a standard menu of songs to the Great British Empire which had to include 'Land of Hope and Glory', 'Oh Canada', 'Eternal Father' and 'I Vow to Thee my Country'. It culminated in each of us giving the Empire three cheers and endless rounds of clapping – the later mainly because we were thrilled to be let off for the afternoon.

Olive Groundwater

version of Sherwood Forest but he wasn't always stealing from the rich! They did eventually capture him each time but he just ran away – he was like Houdini. He was ten years of age when he first ran away and by February 1993 (aged thirteen) he had absconded thirty-five times.

The press couldn't name him until he became over sixteen. He was eventually identified to the world as the 'angel faced' Anthony Kennedy from Springwell Avenue, Walker, and was sent to prison for a good few years in 1997. Life is a bit quieter about the wall these days and presumably will be until he gets released and begins to make nostalgic journeys into the bowels of the heating system again!

Kenny Scott

Ran for his Life

One night the word got around the school that we were going to ambush and beat up a teacher as he came out. It was always difficult to know if these sort of rumours were just bravado or genuine. Anyway, when the time came, quite a big crowd had built up when everyone would normally have been as far as possible away from school. It certainly looked interesting and we, the 'Ayta gang', joined in with the 'Bola gang' – Ayton and Bolam Street kids – to add some weight to the proceedings. By the time the teacher – Mr Foster – came out, it was obvious this was going to be a massacre and before he had stepped out he spun back in and ran for his life to the staff room to phone the police. I heard a whisper that he had upset one of the Malia family – a mistake!

Ken Groundwater

Playing Shops

The street was my second home. I had the freedom of it by right and could come into its full heritage whenever I was able. The part I knew first, the south side, started with a grocer's shop on the corner, ran quite straight past some eighty front doors arranged in twos, one for the upstairs flat, one for the down. Out of school-time several of them would usually be in occupation as the various girl-gangs set up shops or schools in imitation of their elders. I got incorporated in these games, but not very cheerfully after the first time. It was wearing to have to sit still for a long time while Beattie Briggs waved a stick and put on an unpleasant voice with which to simulate teachers: and highly disappointing to have your favourite Nellie Potts lead you to a doorstep set out with empty cocoa tins and sugar packets so that it could call itself a shop and listen to a long dialogue about the price of bacon culminating at last in a series of buys which were mere hollow pretence.

Jack Common

Boody-Stalls

I liked the boody-stalls best. Without warning some fine Saturday morning and by one of those uncalculated and unpremeditated motions which sweep over child-communities, nearly every doorstep would begin to blossom in arrangements of broken glass, china and pebbles. 'Come to my boody-stall,' Annie Smith would call, and the late arrival on the scene would stand awhile admiring the treasure sparkling in the sun, the bits of blue glass, the pink and gold on a segment of china, the ancient sparkle of granite, the leaf gilded upon a lump of coal. Then the newcomer sped away to make her own collection – me helping, perhaps: that's why I liked it. Enormous summers dallied around me as I sat on doorsteps or crawled about warm pavements always with the genial company of my kind close by. I belonged to the street by the same right that I had to belong to one particular family in it. All the livelong day, we were pavement-free and pal-pleasured. Home began again after such a huge interval, with the shouts of mothers calling us in. Few took any notice of that, for a time, except to begin to feel uncomfortable: and presently there'd be a series of aproned descents, rushes, grabs, squawkings and the slam of another door. But often the lamp-lighter was on his rounds before all the small fry were safely back in their boxes.

Jack Common

Raby Street School

I remember I went there shortly after it opened. I hadn't been to school before and I was already nearly seven years old. There were masses of us – there must have been about 400-plus. There was chaos all the time mainly, I seem to recall, due to the small number of real teachers. Remember then you didn't need to be a properly trained teacher. Some older kids were used if they had a bit about them. Extra staff eventually came, though. We were packed like bloody sardines and were deposited all over the place – in every nook and cranny they could find to 'store' us. There seemed to be a lot of unsupervised time where we would get a tutor shoved into our faces and then left to battle through what it meant. One big class must have had nearly eighty in it, as all I can remember was a sea of rickety old desks that sagged quite badly and kids sharing, pushed up tight on the rough plank forms. I believe things did eventually improve.

Willie Harle

Victoria Jubilee School

I started school at Victoria Jubilee in 1913 at the age of five years. All my memories are happy ones. We were poor and hard up, coming as I did from a big family who had

Mister Softee weaves through the back lanes down through Gordon Road to Norfolk Road, 1967. St Lawrence's church steeple is silhouetted before the Felling streets over the river.

very little and were content with the merest necessities of existence.

I made good progress at the school and became a senior in good time. I remember one teacher by the name of Mr Thompson. He taught Standard VI and Mr Hebson was in charge of Standard VII. My favourite in the passing years nevertheless was Miss Goodfellow, who I believe taught Standard IV for the boys. She really was a lovely person and was beloved by all us boys. One of her rules was that any boy who wished unnecessarily to leave the room to wash his hands, could do so on request to Miss Goodfellow, but her condition was that he would get one good strap for going. Of course we all thought it was an honour to be strapped by Miss Goodfellow, who, needless to say, was none too hard on us and always belted us gently with a broad smile on her beautiful face. Any one of the boys would have sacrificed much for her welfare and when the 'belting' was over the entire class was smiling.

Mr Isaac Tunnah, the headmaster, was one of the finest fellows I ever knew and all the boys regarded him with the greatest affection and respect. I remember he lived over in Jesmond Vale and used to walk to school each morning always wearing his 'taily' coat and carrying his umbrella. I cannot ever remember seeing Mr Tunnah wearing an overcoat and he was always delighted when any of his boys met him as he went along and said to him 'Good morning, Sir.'

Possibly some of the elderly ladies of Byker will remember Miss M. Kingham, who was the headmistress of the Senior girls and a grand lady too. She was a disciplinarian but was a fair and lovable person. I knew many of the girls who passed through her hands, including my two sisters, and I never heard an unkind word spoken about her from any of them. She and many others from that time will have passed on, leaving pleasant memories behind.

I know that my name was entered on the large board in the hall known as the 'roll of honour.' I never saw it after I left and would have loved to have seen my name and others I knew. I always had a hankering to pay a visit to the old school and when I did get around to it, alas, the school was no more and the caretaker's house was the only part that remained. Now modern flats have been built right across the site. History had again been made.

We were divided into four main bits. Seniors had the top block, split into girls and boys. The infants and the juniors went further up to the older section of the school. I believe the senior boys bit shut down completely back in 1950 and they were all spread about to the schools of their choice around the newer schools in Byker. The senior girls, however, stuck it out until 1967. This left the younger ones there until the Byker redevelopment swept them away. Its a shame there little to mark the spot. I know it was a grim-looking establishment but think what excellent produce it gave the city on which to grow. Folks should be proud, not bulldozing the site away so happily.

Tommy Burn

Through the Cullie

I was born in Walker Terrace in 1910 and went to Victoria Jubilee Schools. I was the second eldest of a family of eight. Of course, the parents have passed on, but our

Members of the Harle and McClen families enjoy an outing in 1936. Sydney Harle, far right, insisted upon wearing his motor-bike beret at all times. His wife, Cissie, sits behind him, wearing a 1930s sun-hat.

A cartoon from 1975 which appeared in the Byker Phoenix.

Compare the environment for a child at play in 1980 with those earlier scenes. Roses now grow in Byker along the wall! (NCL)

family all knew Byker well. I well remember my pal 'Ginger' and I were looking through the grid at the wash-hoose in Shipley Street once and heard the one of the washer wives say to another: 'Gis' a squeeze of yer blue bag, hinny, and I'll gi' yer a rub of me soap.' Many is the time my pals and me have gone through the 'cullie' [the culvert that ran as a large bore tube through the Ouseburn]. We've gone through it in the pitch black and we've gone through, as many kids did, with a burning bicycle tyre to light it up! The Bridge End 'gym' was a place I well remember and there were some real tough Byker lads got down there. There was George Willis, Benney Sharkey, Jim Falcus, Jimmy Brett and Tom Dusty.

Seaman Watson, who fought for the world title, was another great lad. Fighting in those days was second nature but I will say that you never saw the vandalism that you see today.

Tommy Burn

CHAPTER 2
Home Life

Half-way down Byker Bank and just before Dunn Place was this short cul-de-sac, called Wilkinson's Court. The interesting details on this photograph from around 1930 include a manure pit, newly built wash-house and two outside toilets. (NCL)

Family without Shoes

My mother had friends in Shieldfield, only one of whom had shoes. The entire blooming family was like monkeys. In winter we would sometimes share a pair of shoes but that was back in the '20s. It was like a crazy three-legged thing with a shoe on the farthest feet.

You know in our grannies' time, before the 1890s, the kitchen, living room and the bedroom were all the same thing. There was only one other room and this was the front parlour. It wasn't used unless the Queen or the Vicar was expected!

Aggie Stephenson

Tarmac gives way to granite cobbles, looking down from the short Jane Street to the longer Kendal Street, 1968.

A combined Harrison, McClen and Groundwater family outing into the woods at Dipton with their first car in 1949.

Short Commons

All the times I knew them and visited – which was twice a week at least – this was their only meal: some cheese and bread plus Scots porridge oats. I was often sent for food when me aunty was wanting something quickly and I didn't mind going 'cause of getting some with them – because we didn't have their things to eat at home.

Ken Groundwater

Asking Questions

'Can you get a quarter of Empire Cheese – it must be that cheese mind. Here's half a crown, go to the Co-op: your uncle likes their cheese best and they will have it in. And can you get some sticky milk [Nestlé's milk] and an uncut loaf.' I would return and find them sitting like two children in front of the fire embers. Like as if at fifty years of age they had acknowledged they had nothing else to live for except this sitting by the fire and watching over each other to the background of old Joe's crooning. It was fascinating for me, a seven- or eight-year-old: in a way I attempted to understand in my mind and make sense of their ways. I'd ask a lot of questions that might have wore them down. My questions were tolerated but if I asked anything approaching... anything close to the war when he was still there then Aunty May would say, 'I think ya Mam's wanting you back now.' No fuss – I would simply get up and go and know I had stepped over their line. In the fifties, everything was still war-dominated from the Second World War, but there were many around me who were First World War survivors and it was no mistake how children of the fifties had somewhat war-dominated lives. My father would change into his khaki leggings whenever maintenance work was to be done around the place. We had to keep out of the adults' way when they were working. Adults then made a great play of how this work was 'not for children', unlike today when we share work with the children and are pleased they're interested enough to get away from their computers.

Ken Groundwater

Winter Cold

In winter you didn't want to go out on a night. Besides it being a bit of a luxury, all you craved for was a bit of warmth – that's how basic life was then in the '30s and '40s. these flats were cold. You could get some who would live like paupers – like Scrooge in fact. You could see men cowering around a bank of candles when you went to sell them owt – they wouldn't even buy sticks to light their fires, some of them were so mean. I remember seeing some old body come to the door when I was attempting to make some pennies and she was so much like a huge baggage wrapped in assorted coats and tatters that I hardly knew what I was addressing and simply aimed my questions

Appleton's Buildings led to Ouseburn Road and are mentioned in the text as a community within the greater community on account of their isolation between the rail and road bridges. This view is from 1900. (NCL)

towards the top half of the object. All you got from some were like murmured expletives between colourful language – eh, but they were characters and survivors. Some of the old men looked and smelt the same all winter and a fair bit of the rest of the year too. The old men who lived alone all looked the same, like Wilfred Bramble – you know, Steptoe. They had the same scowling curse permanently upon the lips especially when we had a particularly bad winter , such as '41, '47, '49. It nearly always snowed through the Januaries in the forties.

Going out on a night was unusual in winter then. We huddled together close to the warmth from the kitchen – that's if we could get near for the other members of the family with same idea. The steam of our mam's baking or from the ever-boiling kettle were like honey to us kids. Mams had to bake then and the warmth when you had your own gas cooker was marvellous. Before we got the cooker me mother used to make up the dough and us kids used to take it up to a Shields Road bakers – I forget the name – and pay him a penny for him to bake it in his big oven. Aah... the smell when it came out and the heat of it was marvellous. We used to take our time going back home and just luxuriate in the heat and the smell. Simple things then that we take no notice of now.

When she got her own cooker it was great 'cause she let us make up our own pastry men with any leftover dough. That and the fun and the warmth made the kitchen a place nobody wanted ever to leave then. You remember these times better than the bad times. How we used to talk and laugh, all us kids around her pinny. We then thought we were rich – you know? It was all we could want then: warmth and friendly banter. As a say, simple basic wants. There

was none of this want, want, want all the time that we get these days in the rush to keep up with them down the street.

Olive Lawrence

Bedtime Rituals

Me mother did the same things with her granny around their even older black leaded range before the days of your own cooker or owt like that. Anyway we didn't want a lot and didn't go out much after seven or eight on a night, what with the cold and the lack of pennies. Every other room in the house was like ice. Going to bed was a major exercise in itself and something that had to be planned out in military fashion. It was everyone's terror being left up last with no heat anywhere! What we'd do to start was all the girls started off in the kitchen with a bit of privacy from the lads. We'd strip off and douse ourselves whilst stood in a tin bath – one at a time whilst our mam would keep boiling up more water and adding to the steam and mayhem. If Mam was too busy or not looking we'd pretend to use the carbolic soap but would just splash the cloth all over and hurry into the warm towel pleased to have survived without too many icicles. She would often insist that we each sat down in it at least five minutes to get well covered, and then out and 'next please!' sort of thing. Our Bella was the oldest and biggest and always got in foggy [first]. We used to giggle when she started to get hair – you know – in funny places and we would tease her about turning into a monkey and stuff like that. She started going in last 'cause of this, and our mother would chase us so Bella could have a bit privacy. Until, that is, we all got some like her. The lads were next and would make any excuse to get a cheap thrill through any cracks in the door but it was all a good laugh and we lasses did the same to them. It was all very innocent stuff, mind. We all knew each other very well and knew all our own little traits and would always be teasing each other them. The race to get to bed was sped up whenever we were hanging the bag by Mam saying something like, 'Hark! I can hear yer father coming!' We didn't half move then!

Fathers were always last in and often quite late in then but, as I say, we really went willingly enough because of the cold and that. We got into bed with socks and jumpers to start with on the very cold nights so's you could gradually warm up. These bedrooms were like ice boxes and the bed sheets nothing like now but more like cardboard. The only soft thing was the eiderdown top or the collection of proggie mat-like covers put on to get some more weight. Some of us kids had like patchwork quilts over us. Pillows were often just a case stuffed with jumpers. We would stay right under for ages until almost expiring with lack of air until the freezing got better or we simply got used to it. Gradually after about half an hour the heads started re-appearing. For devilment we would pop off our socks and place our feet on some delicate part of our sister. The shriek brought our mam in. Feet were always a problem; they were always clammy and freezing. We would sometimes start a bed-kicking match just to warm them up and it was times like this that I was pleased I was in with me sisters! The noise would always get us into trouble and we would be told that the neighbours were knocking through. There was real respect for neighbours and we would have died if they had said that they had heard us next day.

Olive Lawrence

Violet Groundwater, Billy McClen and his adoptive mother May in Welbeck Road, 1933. In 1938, Billy, emigrated to Australia and never saw the shores of 'auld blighty' again.

Getting Up

There was one thing worse than going to bed and that was getting out of it again! You spent half the night warming up and when you had just got warm and comfy you got shouted up and had to begin the whole thing in reverse! It was worse than committing suicide was the prospect of getting out. I used to put me clothes on after dragging them up through the bed. I was warm but looked like some sort of concertina.

Aggie Stephenson

A cartoon *from the* Byker Phoenix.

Looking After Each Other

They had a lot to put up with. Their man would come in on a Thursday and when he'd had his tea he'd say, 'There y'are, Peggie: that's all I can manage this week, pet, but we should be gettin' a bonus or summat soon. We would know there was a good bit taken out of what he'd got. I was lucky, my man was in reg'lar work. Me friend at number 42 had no such luck. She'd tell us sometimes he'd brought nowt at all back yerm [home]. It wasn't that common, mind. We would all help each other out. I remember we did a whip-round in the hairdressers once when we found out that that Nellie Robson had got nowt for the second week running and her with two bairns to feed. She was getting like a waif,

so's we had this collection and got about £2 and left it in an envelope on her kitchen drainer with a note saying it had been found in her backyard and was rightfully hers an' all. You knows she wouldn't have taken it if we'd telt her. She was right proud. It was almost always done like that between ourselves. We were like an unofficial club, tha knows. We would get to hear by whispers that such an' such was on hard times and hadn't turned out for ages. 'Ee, I haven't seen Betty for days – is she all reet?' This would set the ball rolling. Somebody else might chip in with 'Ee, I heard the cutlery stottin' off the walls a bit back. Ee, you've got me worried noo, Bella... I hope she's all reet?'

Nellie Avison

Cold Conditions

n coldest winter you didn't want to go out
on a night', it being a bit of a luxury when
ll you craved for a bit of warmth and food.
These Tyneside flats worked on the basis
hat the communal heat crossed all
nternal dividing walls and thus we shared
ur warmth sideways and especially
pwards. An upstairs flat was desirable in
winter! But they were still cold. There
vere some who lived like paupers and very
nuch like Scrooge. You would glimpse
hem cowering behind their candle using

Alex and Violet Groundwater in 1919, with children Ivy and Stan. They are at 96 Ayton Street, the home of Michael and Alice Harle.

The author is blinded as sun penetrates the murk of Byker in a typical back-lane sun trap, 1953.

the light to read the *Chronicle* to see who
had died and to rejoice in their living
death! When we kids went around the
doors to sell them owt we got no joy as
some, like old Mr Leadbitter, wouldn't
even light a fire and consequently wasn't
interested in buying our bundle of sticks (a
bargain for twopence). Some of the old
men looked the same all year round and
carried their stale smell with them on the
daily trod in and out of the Co-op!

Stan Groundwater

Another view of the rear of 96 Ayton Street in 1919. The matriarch of the family, Alice, is sitting centre-stage next to her husband, Michael Harle. Three generations of the family are around her – her sons and their wives behind, grandchildren in front. On 14 April 1934 Michael died and Alice fell ill immediately, saying, 'I want to be with Michael.' She died three days later. It was one of Newcastle's biggest double funerals. Michael was a reputable joiner for Newcastle Corporation and was well respected.

The Kitchen Range

The heat from our Mam's baking or the steam constantly oozing from the ever-boiling kettle hob was like honey to us. She had to bake and the warmth made for more friendly conditions, conditions that encouraged her to want to chat and were favourable to conviviality – that's when we swapped our tales or family lore and legend. We knew she did the same with her granny because she would tell us what they chatted about, but in her day there was a difference and the difference centred on the mode of cooking. She would tell us that they were never far away from the black range that devoured most of the wall width around the fire in their living room. She would say that she and her eight brothers and sisters would often sleep on the floor at the foot of the range when the drapes in the rest of the house were iced up. Our relations, the Harles, had an older property and still had a black leaded range. It consisted of the main fire area around which were several pockets for different functions – all needing some form of heat in varying degrees of intensity. The range worked by the main oven being right above the fire and secondary ovens/storage areas nearby where food could stand. One of these was ideal for dough to rise in and the range was designed very definitely with bread in mind. This was before the gas cooker migrated into a place called the kitchenette and took us all in with it!

Olive Lawrence

Home Dentist

We were only little 'uns when me mam says: 'Youse lot better be on ya best behaviour this Thursday 'cause the dentist is coming. If he catches ya giving it welly I cannot say what he might do.' This had us thinking what he might do! We speculated for most of the five days before the Saturday but had our imaginations running wild. We didn't even know what he did exactly, being only five-ish.

The day came and me mother rounds us all up from playing with dead ash in the fire grate, saying: 'Right, youse – you're all going into the parlour and if I hear so much as a squeak I'll let the dentist loose on youse – so's you're warned!' Now this was a turn up for the books. She was letting us loose in the best room where Dad's best clothes were hidden *and* she was leaving us alone there.

Anyways, the front door knocker goes about ten minutes later and sounds of large feet go past our door with us straining a view through the gap but just seeing passing black. 'What's he going to do with Peter and Ian?' us little 'uns wonder. Peter and Ian were the oldest two of the six of us, see.

Eventually sounds from the living room indicate that furniture is being moved about

Left: *The author's mother in grey wartime garb, pictured at Jerome's Studios on Shields Road in 1940.*
Right: *The author's father looking serious as he has his portrait taken on Shields Road before setting off for war in 1939.*

and the big table sounds like it's being dragged over the floor. We don't like this one bit and tell each other that maybe Peter and Ian have been very bad. Well you could guess what happens. We make a noise 'cause we're frightened being alone in this scary polished room where Granny was laid out, and me mother comes in and sees us all blubbing and asking, 'Is Peter and Ian being killed?' and so on. She starts laughing and throws up her apron like she did when amused and says, 'Why, no, pets!' and adds, 'Come and look.'

When we got in what had happened was that the dentist had purloined the big dining table, pulling it over to be nearer the light from the window, and was using it as his operating table with both Peter and Ian laid flat out with things stuck out of their mouths. We were pleased to see them alive, I'll tell ya!

Pat Dinning

Bathing and Washing

To get bathed was an achievement in itself. First you had to board up the scullery window, then you had to drag out the bungalow bath onto the stone floor. Finally, every large pan in the house had to be filled with water and placed upon the gas. Wash-day was no easier. The water had to be boiled in an enormous cast-iron pot, surrounded by brickwork and heated underneath by an open fire in the grate. The clothes were dropped into the water and beaten with a large poss-stick. When clean, the excess water was run off using a hand-operated mangle. Those were the days!

John Bonner

Bad Lots

Certain families you know to be evil, like. I divn't want to name names but you knew to keep oot their way.

Joe McCler

Broken Boilers

My main complaint is the heating in the houses. The thermo-couplers in the boiler-room keep breaking. Sometimes when I've reported the fault to the council, I've been told that there was no engineer on duty. When this happens and it's freezing cold I take it upon myself to break into the boiler room and restart the gubbins myself!

Jack Hooper

Early Consumer Goods

My grandma got a 'Servis' washing machine in 1955 and I think that was the first one I'd seen in Byker. Grandma got Rediffusion installed sometime early in the fifties. It must have been about 1956 because it had selections on the bakelite brown controller fixed to the windowsill for TV channels. It had the selections marked from A to G around the circumference and the four radio channels were on there. I think she later got another ontroller when the extra channels came in marked from 1 to 10. My uncle was keen on DIY and loved going to J.T. Dove's to get stuff.

Ken Groundwater

Old Superstitions

The people still have that countryman's tight sense of village loyalty, only in Byker their village consists of small groups of streets in which they were born and in which they have stayed. Byker, to each of them, is only those streets they know intimately. One and all know that Byker Bank is really heartland Byker. Along with this rural thinking goes all the superstitions which have long disappeared elsewhere. This is an example: A woman who has a child must be 'churched' before she is acceptable as a visitor to another home. This attitude goes back long before Christianity. Babies and marriages are at the

The tin bath awaits duty on the outside of No. 168 Albion Row in the heartland of Byker, 1964. The shared back-yard door has the numbers (166 and 168) of both upstairs and downstairs flats. (NCL)

It's washing-day Monday in Byker, 1968.

centre of superstition. As a family sets off for church for the baptism of a baby they carry with them a parcel to be given to the first person they meet of the opposite sex to the new baby. The parcels are known variously as the 'alms' or the 'bread and cheese' and they usually contain scones or a teacake with a silver coin in. Some mean folk might have a silver threepence piece inside, which wasn't quite in the true spirit of the custom; nevertheless, it qualified. The customs continued when out with the new-born and shopping along Shields Road. When the child baptised to make it thrive.

At weddings a slightly dangerous custom was to have the bride walking on a golden coin which resulted in the 'hoy-out' Intended to appease evil spirits, the hoy-out became more like an appeasement of the local kids. They would gather around as the happy couple were about to drive away and shout 'hoy-out!' The couple must then scatter coins into the air. The kids would fight across the road to get the most of this rich picking, and it was a useful source to add to slim funds if you lived a handy distance from the church.

Joan Elliot

Christmas

Christmas Day was the one time when I could do no wrong. This was the only time (apart from funerals) when I got a taste of the way life was in my dad's diaries. It was old fashioned thirties get-togethers when the adults dropped their guard and I got to taste strong liquid without a scolding. The old 'uns would arrive – old Auntie May and Uncle Joe and a host of Harle relations that I only saw occasionally, plus Aunt Lizzie with strange twisted legs like my Grandma and Harrison relations of Auntie Ivy and Uncle Charlie. On Christmas morning I would lead a comical procession up and down the living room beating out time to encourage the 'cooks' (my mother and aunts) to work even harder. I remember the first time I did this I was surprised to see the older men joining in. It must have been the 'regimental' instruction they had had, but thereafter each Christmas we marched up and down with anything that made a noise and mostly the kit from off the front of the

St Peter's allotments allowed the menfolk of Byker their own indulgences while presenting a scenic Felling shoreline. They are seen here in 1968.

pram joined all the others lined up outside the shop, passers-by would feel it would be bad luck for them to pass by without dropping some silver onto the clothing. Upon returning home the mother would find a small shower of silver coins raining down when tidying the pram. It wasn't abnormal to find it amounted to £2, not an inconsiderable amount in the 1950s, and all for an hour's shopping, more, in fact than you had spent on the groceries. It was considered bad luck to put the baby in short clothes before it was baptised and many an otherwise non-churchgoing family has had a

Rainer's Portrait Studio on Shields Road attracted the attention of the author's Orcadian great-grandfather, James Groundwater, in around 1899. His serious 'brood' includes the author's great-uncle James (top left) and grandfather Alex (top right). James Groundwater Snr migrated from the island of Hoy to St Peter's Road in Byker via his first port of call, Woodbine Street in South Shields.

From left to right, Hilda and Evelyn Marriott and Olive Groundwater congregate ready for the 'hoy-out' at the wedding of Ivy Groundwater and Charles Harrison, at Byker parish church in 1936.

fire. This was the high point of too many low points in a grey workaday Byker world. You remember these days forever and quickly learn to dismiss those grim times. The Christmas period up to the end of Boxing Day was a never ending stream of visits from distant relations but mainly with Harle family connections. Peggy and Frank Johnson, who lived next door to Pop in Ayton Street, were exceptional good value and had all the womenfolk in hoots until they had to make dashes to the loo. Peggy was constantly in a high degree of emotion over something or other. This was a surprise to me to meet such theatrical people without many inhibitions and I was fascinated at this behaviour. Before long she was doing a not-so-modest 'can-can' with my mother. This was brilliant, I thought, whilst also cowering around the back of chairs amazed at the extravagance of it all but not daring to miss the slightest sight of this peek-show – and nobody cared!

Eventually Peg's daughter would turn up. Now this was heaven to an inquisitive seven-year-old! She was the closest thing to Miss World a raggy-arsed kid from Byker had yet to see. She could (and did) sing sublimely, with all the actions. Plus add to this the illegal alcohol consumption and I was as near as I could be to Heaven. If her daughter – Vera – even just looked at me then that was me struggling not to let my obvious interest take over and wreathed in a very hot red face. If this was an insight into how families and friends enjoyed themselves through the thirties then I was disappointed that the TV had come along –providing we could keep it only for footie and *Popeye*!

The culmination of Christmas was my cousin Douglas's new girlfriend singing the show song 'Cock-eyed Optimist'. I thought I was at the Palladium after that rendering and fell head-over-heels in love with her. Lucky cousin Douglas! Those moments stay with you forever when you looked out onto tomorrow's mean streets outside and caught a glimpse of a drunk trying to aim himself roughly towards his home.

There was always some vitriolic old battle-axe that would get in on the proceedings and, depressed with the drink, would misunderstand the proceedings and, true to type, begin to outpour her wisdom with such as 'We all have a bitter cup to drink, hinny: it's poured out for us before we're born.'

Ken Groundwater

42

Christmas Parcels

This is a transcription of a letter sent by an unemployed man, Mr B. Maw, asking to be considered for one of Lipton's 'Christmas parcels', given out to needy families to tide them over the festive season. It was written during the recession of the early 1920s, following the First World War, when many soldiers were demobbed only to find themselves facing indefinite unemployment.

From Mr B. Maw, 223 Kendal Street, Byker, Newcastle.
Dec. 9th, 1922.

Sir,
I beg to make application for a Xmas Parcel from Liptons. My Income is 33/- per week, £1-2-0 from Labour Exchange and 11/- from the Guardians. I am paying ten shillings for rent of a Combined Room, 4/- for coal, 1/2 for Gas and a 1/- for a ticket, that leaves 16/10 to keep four of us on for a week. I'm a married man with two children and have been out of work for close on 12 Months now. I also wish to state that I have dealt with Liptons for years and have been a good Customer to them, so I trust you will give this my application your kindest consideration.

Thanking you in anticipation, I am Your Obedient Servant, Sir,

Mr B. Maw

Musical Memories

I used to go into their house in Ayton Street and listen quietly to his sad songs. They were a lot like his anthem. He would quietly hum a war years dirge. God only knows where he really was in his mind. He would just sit there and stare out of these sunken gas-damaged eyes, and hum away the themes that we knew were favourites of the First World War years. When Aunty May was getting a bit sick of his mistakes, like the time he brought the wrong cheese back, she would get ratty with him. He would simply start singing: 'Darling we are getting older…silver threads among the gold…' and so on. It was as if nothing could get to him after what he had witnessed. I was wary of him and would sometimes follow him along to the shops to see what he got up to, but he didn't… – he was harmless.

Ken Groundwater

Stan Groundwater on a friends Sunbeam motorbike at Blanchland in 1934.

Ivy Groundwater (centre; subsequently Harrison) became a piano teacher working from home in Ayton Street. With her here in Bacon's studio on Shields Road are her son and daughter Moyra and Douglas in 1941.

Ration of Mince

We had our favourite 'ration' of food, as she would call it: it was our main meal all the time, our two ounces of mince.

May McClen

Food in the 1940s

British beef was expensive in the 1940s and 1950s and we had to often make do with imported Argentinian beef. It cost about 2s 6d for a piece of meat for Sunday roast including a bit of dripping to cook it in. When we saw it come out of the deep freezer it was a deep purple colour. 'Jellied veil' was a favourite of the pensioners, although they would buy only about 2oz or the same amount of mince. Unpackaged food abounded. Butter and cheese were straight out of their barrels. Empire cheese was reasonably cheap, was red and sweated with a soapy look. Cheddar and Cheshire were expensive if you saw them available but it was likely that you had to go over 'town' [Newcastle] and to Fenwick's to get delicatessen.

('Jellied veil' (or veal) was softened calf-meat often prescribed by doctors for those with 'delicate' stomachs.)

Pauline Davidson

Glendinning's famous pawnbroker's shop was run by three generations of the family.

45

CHAPTER 3
Street Life

Aramaic of Southampton deposits her wares at the quayside extension, the construction of which was overseen by foreman joiner Alex Groundwater. This brought a piece of quay right up to the end of Glasshouse Street (which continued upwards as Raby Street) In this 1957 view, Raby Street is on the right, leading towards Byker parish church, high on the hill. Spiller's flour mill is dominant to the left. (Courtesy of the Port of Tyne)

Along the River

We often drifted down to the river, but not living alongside it, we weren't encouraged or needed to be good swimmers. We mainly went down there to frighten ourselves. We knew the sheds were crawling with foreigners and really hard cut-throat types taking on any work going. We called them black-dogs, pirates and suchlike names and would creep around the sides and the backs of the sheds like we thought the police did and crept up upon the ship-side action where we definitely weren't allowed. We could see

46

Although mysterious and inhospitable, the Quayside sheds were nevertheless a great attraction to marauding Byker lads through the ages.

them engrossed in their work and rarely thought we had been seen – how naïve we were! On one occasion they allowed us to get so far into the shed and around the back of barrels and boxes and stuff, then suddenly decided to close those great shed doors and shout knocking-off time etc. Well you should have seen us go! That really taught us a lesson. They were like hawks and never missed a trick, those dockers. They knew every trick themselves, I suppose.

Frankie Johnson

Pirates on the River

Other times we simply went down to the river to watch the ships. This would invariably terrify us in a different way when the crews going past would shout blood-curdling things at us. One ship was full of what we thought were pirates. They shouted that when they docked they would come and get us and slit our throats. When one really nasty looking character said he would jump over and made out to swim at us, we fled. Now I come to think about it, we never stayed long near the river such was the grim shapes and natural dangers thereabouts. It's funny, but I never heard of any of us kids being drowned, maybes this was to do with this natural fear. The ships then were an awful size, especially when the river was high and all we kids could see was this metal slab-sided wall covered in rust and green slime and such stuff. When we were lurking about and one of the steamships let off a steam whistle then you should have seen us fly. We thought we'd been spotted and it was a signal to capture us – such were our childish minds.

One day we saw a steam tug trying to turn another larger vessel – it might have been a Danish one 'cause it was white – and it was having terrible difficulty getting it around against the swell and a strong wind running. We watched in silent amazement, the plucky little tug got deeper and deeper into the water at its stern as it fought against the wind and the strong running tide. It pulled and pulled and eventually the stern was under water with the tug over at a crazy angle pulling like hell. We couldn't take our fascinated eyes away from this spectacle of what we thought was certain disaster but we had always wanted to see a ship sunk as we had heard such terrible things about what happens to the men. Just when we knew it must sink the big ship started to swing. I'm not certain if it was a major disappointment but we were spared the details. We went home rehearsing what we would tell our Mams and dads and by home, had decided to say it had sunk but bobbed up again and was

The Fossway/Shields Road industrial area in 1966. The railway had private siding links into all these places, especially for Parsons and Metal Box. This coal train is passing Heaton loco sheds at which Jack Common's father worked.

A glimpse of the St Peter's shoreline shows us the butt of musical hall jokes that refer to Byker Sands! A riverside diesel stands at St Peter's station alongside the giant cranes of Shepherd's scrap-yard complex in July 1969.

OK. This was better than saying nothing actually happened.

Ernie Neil

Byker Sands

The pigeon lofts along the river were difficult for us kids to get into. There were few opportunities for getting through the back-door planking that generally made up the perimeter construction. We would listen to the old gadgies inside billing and cooing to their birds and thought they were off their rockers. We would mimic them but got tired of this and would drift further down to the railway that ran on the river's edge above a bit of green rocky slime covered shoreline that we laughingly called Byker Sands! Whether this was in fact the Byker Sands that was made immortal hereabouts via the likes of Bobby Thompson [a well-known local comedian] I can't be certain, but it was the nearest shoreline to Byker and was tight between St Peter's and Bird's Nest.

Frankie Johnson

Car Pushing

The winters were bad in the fifties. We nearly always had a long white period when the steep banks in Byker were better than being in Austria – until that is some old crow came out and sprinkled hearth ashes out of her fire onto the 'runs' when we were at school. They were treacherous to the old people, though. Anyway, we saw this black Ford. In these winters it was a waste of time having a car. It got to the foot of Commercial Road and stuck there after many attempts to get up. Well they then took it around to Ayton Street to try there – it was, if anything, worse. The car spent the next week marooned at the foot of the bank while we sledged from schooltime till bedtime trying to go under it and all – it was brilliant and freezing. We finally got it back up the bank on the next Saturday tea-time. What happened, happened in an instant, we had begun to slowly push up the bank when someone shouted 'How-way, gis a hand to get it up the bank!' and everyone descended – even some grown ups out of the shadow of doorways. It was mad really in those days but that's the way things happened. It was anything for a challenge and a game. There wasn't enough space on the car for all the hands and when we got it to St Peter's Road we were all cheering madly and loudly and more and more wanted to join in this game. I swear we could have pushed that car to North Shields and back before supper, such was the energy and enthusiasm of the moment and that's how it was then. There was no bad feeling or owt like that.

Nellie Avison

Alley Football

Through stubborn brown plasticine, cheesy milk bottle rims and the smell of Izaal we dreamt and fooled away the years until we went to junior school. Here we huddled in terror for the majority of the first year to avoid the streetwise practical jokers eager to prey on our soft white skin. These ten- or eleven-year-old 'maniacs' were only too soon to become ourselves. Ah, but there was one escape from this oppression and that was to excel in a sport that would set you apart and add a face to your features at an premature age. Football, it was said, was the opium of the masses before today's drug craze hit the streetwise. It certainly was the opium to us little kids. To be half descent at 'footie' was the dream and to attain this get-out we would not just *train* (by today's understanding of the word) but we would play and play and run ourselves ragged. We would play footie all night if we could.

A wonderful feel for the communal 'ambience' of the narrow Byker back lanes is evident in this 1957 aerial view over Shields Road off Robinson Street. (NCL)

'A footie game would last all the day.' Norfolk Road with access via a hole in the mesh, 1973.

The back-lanes, to begin with, were our theatre and the back-lane doors were hammered mercilessly until the damage was detected and we moved on up to Mrs Kilroy's door, and so on, until most cats and dogs had 'natural' flaps to escape from their own back-yard imprisonment. In the yard at each break time a footie game was started when we still had our jackets on and they, flying behind like sails, assisted our passage. The ball was anything from a crab-apple, the inevitable tin-can, through to used exercise books and (and this was real luxury) ...a tennis ball thieved from the girls! The game broke up when the ball broke up!

Ken Groundwater

Running Errands

If the winter was bad our mams would say, 'Go and ask auld Mrs Cannybody if she needs owt down at Chadwick's or wherever.' We didn't worry about the door being shut but would just bellow in through the letter-box: 'Mrs, do you want owt down at Chadwick's shop 'cause I'm gannin' for me mam.' Old Peggie Davison would be stubborn and eventually gan out herself, but she wouldn't change her clothes just 'cause it was a bit icy – nee way. She would gan out in her same clathes [clothes] whatever the event or weather. She'd come out in the same old shawl and broon frock but what got me was the fact that she'd have on her ancient battered slippers. You know the sort, everybody's granny had them then. They had this bit of fur around the opening and a silly bobbly thing stuck on the top. Sometimes the bobble was tartan and looked plain ridiculous but it was like an old body's standard bit of kit then. Anyway, Peggie would end up dragging these daft slippers through the snow and clarts and slush, like they were bulldozer ploughs with this daft thing bobbin' away on the front and us kids falling about and pointing to them. I think of these old characters and know we will never see then again except in comic cartoons like 'the Broons'.

Nellie Avison

Sociable Streets

We all shared each other's ups and downs, births, deaths and bereavements. We saved for weeks and weeks for a bus trip. I can still remember one return from Seaburn on a darkened coach listening to the harmonies of the Inkspots crooning over the charabanc radio.

Two streets shared a back lane and sports were arranged between the two, handicaps worked out and prizes awarded and a tea party laid out by the womenfolk on a long table in the back-lane. These back-lanes were worn and torn and in constant need of resurfacing especially after bonfire night.

The bonfire! Timber was collected and stored for weeks beforehand, often in the many air-raid shelters that littered the vicinity. Old chairs were donated, redundant rabbit hutches, old lino – in fact anything that was transportable and inflammable. On the night, everyone was out. People stood by and watched, some holding candles or home-made lanterns, some with ARP stirrup pumps and water buckets – ready to douse down the smouldering back door. Then there were the potatoes, shoved in the embers and roasted. Bonfire night was a marvellous occasion.

John Bonner

Staple Diets

I remember the litter-free streets and the milky-cream key-stoned doorsteps at every door along the streets. There were net curtains and aspidistras at every window. There was plenty of life in Byker's back lanes. The girls played hopscotch on the narrow pavements. This was in the twenties. There was a constant procession of horses and carts. Milkmen came round and sold milk from churns and housewives took their jugs out. Then came the

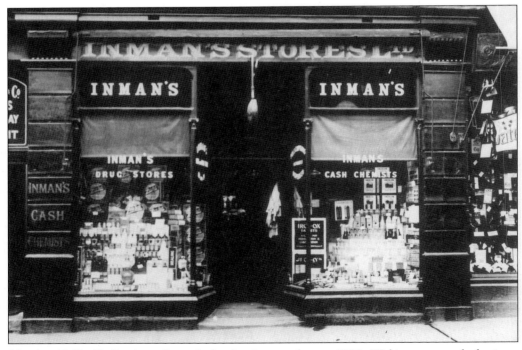

Number 19 Shields Road was Inman's the chemist, seen here c. 1900. Within ten years the business would be swallowed up and become a small part of a much bigger Boots the Chemist. (NCL)

Neighbours greet and chat for a while on Shields Road, 1972. A similar scene has occurred every day since 1880 in this heartland of meetings for Byker people. The posters to the right of Dennison and Graham's chemists show that the Apollo Cinema was running two films: Shaft's Big Scare *and* 2001: A Space Odyssey. *(NCL)*

Queues for the bus build up on both sides of the road in front of Parrish's Store on Shields Road, 1974. (NCL)

As shown here, Welbeck Road grew in a more piecemeal fashion than most areas of Byker. Here two hired traps make their slow way towards Shields Road on 18 June 1901, with several areas of wasteland and old mines prominent. (NCL)

fishmonger, the fruit and veg cart. Food then was cheap and plentiful. Oranges and fresh herrings were four for one old penny. We thrived on them and stotty cake. Scotch broth and Irish stew – that was the staple diet of Byker folk. If Monday was washing day then Tuesday was baking day. Nearly every housewife baked her own bread and cakes in a large heavily black-leaded oven and placed them to cool on a table by the open window. The smell was delicious. Life then centred on Headlam Street. Old Byker village had been pulled down and a new park created, it was always packed with happy noisy youngsters.

Louise Toomer

Country Byker

It was all fields beyond the top of Shields [Road] when I first came. I loved it 'cause there was so much I could do when I was little. The quarries were still there as well and we could get lost in them from morn till neet. I loved it then. It was like it was split in to country Byker and street Byker. Youse lot on'y saw it lined with hooses! There was even a farm where me Aunt Ina went for milk. I thinks it was doon Welbeck Road way. I can certainly remember coos doon there.

Willie Harle

The Harle branch of the author's Byker background. Here is Robbie Harle and wife plus son Brian and his own family.

In the Pits

Me mates would play some evil tricks on unsuspecting young 'uns that came near the quarry. You know, like not too bad or anything, but quite scary for the young 'uns. They would lie in wait and when the young 'uns came along would hurl them down into the pits. It was soft ground but they would keep them there until they got tired of the sport and let them go after they had made them do all sorts – like walk around on all fours and such-like. There was some who were evil, like. Some wouldn't let them oot till they were red with crying – you knows. We kept clear of them sorts, like, me and me pals.

Robbie Harle

Summer Nights

The best neets were in summer. All the mams got out into the lane and stood there with folded arms, like, all agreeing and looking friendly to us kids and relishing a bit of heat and no work to do. They would say stuff like: 'Eh, Aggie, your Philip's growing and all. Is he owt of them shoes you got him last summer already?' And: 'I love his Fair Isle jumper.... Ee, I'd love one for our Billy.'

Aggie Stephenson

Spring Evenings

After the cold weather the very first warm evening would bring them all out as if it were some celebration of surviving another winter. The street games were restricted to what you could get up to in the narrow width of the back-lane. Skipping was perfect and all the kids joined in – even the mothers, when they were wanting to be a bit exhibitionist, and all. Fathers were seen but generally skulked in their dark overalls and were often too exhausted to even speak after a shift.

Robbie Harle

Playing Doors

The lads would play 'doors' but some neighbours would get upset to hear their doors being crashed against again and again and would eventually come out and let

bleeze with a mouthful. They didn't negotiate or owt as they might today but simple boiled over and said, 'I've had enough, now that's it. Clear off, Mickey – I knows yer dad's got a temper,' and so on, and they'd use these type of threats and they'd know that it would work – unless you were one of those without a father and then you could do what you liked. They were generally the cheekiest kids.

Stephen Maine

Hawkers' Cries

I remember the street traders' cries.... Some cries that still stand out were: 'Sticks-oh, diddy-oh, sticks-oh' from the woman selling firewood and herself resembling a bundle of rags.

The Harrisons and Groundwaters stop for a smoke out in the countryside of Matfen in 1933.

A dank Sunday morning in 1967 catches Bolam Street folk on the move. The well-known Morris's 'chippie' is on view above the last parked car at the top on the right in St Peter's Road.

'Calla Herrin' from the fresh herring-wifies from the coast.

'Any ole lumber' – the rag and bone man.

'Co-al, co-al!' – the coal seller (with variations, as there were quite a few came round).

'Chro-o-nick! Evening Chronicle!' from the lads sent out from Sandy's newsagent when they weren't selling so well.

'Footba-a-a-l ... Fina-a-l!' from the lad selling the Saturday-only *Football Pink*.

Rita Richardson

Shops Remembered

Some shops along Shields Road have hardly ever changed in all the times I've been shopping there and that's since the early 1930s. Some shops that must have been there thirty years or longer were: Tomm's the cycle dealer, W's hosiery shop, Carrick's cake shop, Pledger's drapers, Bookless the fruiterer. There were Freeman's and Scallon's next to each other. We could get smashing ice cream at Risi's near the bottom of Shields Road.

There was always plenty of choice when it came to pawnbrokers. There were Moore's, Niman's, and John Gledinning's down Raby Street. We were spoilt for confectionery shops around the top of Shields Road and it may have been something to do with Watson's Toffee Factory being in the vicinity! This was in Union Road, close to the Bamborough Cinema. We were spoilt for choice also when it came to cinemas. There was the Brinkburn, the Imperial, the Scala – along Chillingham Road – and the Sun. The Sun didn't last too long. Also the Grand Theatre, Byker. Quite a choice if you had the money!

There were some odd combinations and in Dalton Street the Royal Station pub was bang next to a cat-meat supplier. Strange smells used to permeate up Conyers Road. They had a pawnbrokers close to the pub which was very handy in those days. The bottom end of Shields Road was furniture and butcher land. There must have been a dozen furniture businesses; Beaven's, Gillis', Young's and Wike's are some I recall, but there were many more. Then there were countless butchers. I recall Dodd's, Sawyer's, Flounder's and Dewhurst's, and Dodd's had more than one shop on the go. There was even a Butcher's Arms pub. Our favourite place of all had to be Woolworth's and the variety of items they had. The Rediffusion shop was near the Buttercup Dairy – some names you can never forget.

Rita Henderson

The Raby Bingo

Edward Davison was manager of the bingo from 1961 to 1979.

On Christmas Eve 1958 Jimmy Clavering and I assemble Christopher's present from Santa Claus, a model railway, on the big room table. It worked perfectly and as we played with it we discussed the future. We knew in our hearts the cinema was doomed.

A family gathering at South Shields pier in 1938 to celebrate the twenty-first birthday of Walter Fell.

1948. Looking up Raby Street from a point on Walker Road. The No. 19 'Walker Circular' bus is on a tram replacement service – the overhead wires are evident. On the right is Elizabeth and Annie Simpson's grocery store which was extant in the early 1960s. A faded 'Lambs Ales & Stout' sign is evidences of a previous era. The 'Bottom Club' is on the left. (NCL)

Grafton Street meets Shields Road, 1973. Among the familiar-sounding shops is the now taken-over Walker and Byker Building Society. (NCL)

What was going to happen to the Brighton, the Plaza, the Rex and others under Jimmy's control? I myself being involved with fifty cinemas couldn't face forced retirement at fifty-three years of age. The cinemas closed one by one and another year goes by. A fort and a ship for Christopher. Before he got his ship I painted my wife's name on it for good luck: 'Babs'. He still has it to this day.

Alfred Shepherd (Jimmy's uncle) and I, together with Colin Buglass, were invited to the Grand Opening of Bingo at the Oxford Galleries. After the session 'we three' decided that Bingo was our salvation, so Alfie opened the Heaton, I opened the Raby Bingo and Colin the Gloria. Alfie was a very great friend of mine and although we were in opposition we saw each other every day and over a coffee would talk bingo. Eventually Alfie and Colin retired and when they died I certainly lost two sincere friends. Actually Alfie had invited Babs and me up to Seahouses for a holiday, but it was not to be.

Jimmy and Christopher now run the Heaton, and when Christopher was a boy he said to me one day 'Mr Davison, when I grow old can I buy the Raby?' I said, 'Certainly Chris, you save your pocket money and one day the Raby will be yours.' Chris said, 'Cross your heart and hope to die,' and I said ' So be it.'

Edward Davison

Raby Street

Then we had Raby Street for other things. There were even more butchers along here, maybe twenty-plus. Hooper's chemist had been there years, as had Humpish the butcher. Humpish was our family's favourite.

I think every family in Byker stuck to a certain butcher until they got an over-fatty bit of bacon and tried another and so on until you had tried all thirty in the area and began again. Violet used to send an order into Stanley Everett's the grocers who set up lower down Raby Street – towards the bottom club. In the late fifties, past Everett's was the Red Stamp Stores. It was sort of like a precursor to the Green Shield Stamp fad that got hold of everyone in the sixties which Kensitas cigarettes did very well out of. Everett's would deliver for a few pennies more and that was quite posh then. Near the Co-op butchers on the other side near the top was Barsanti's who had unusual clothes. Pop and Charlie sometimes used to get seeds from Henderson, a short way past another pawnbrokers who name I've forgotten. We still called it Henderson's in spite of its

Lowrie's egg factory provides a full-stop to Harbottle Street on a wet August day in 1973.

Waiting for a call as the tension mounts in the Raby Bingo Hall (otherwise known as 'the coffin'), 1975. (Courtesy of Sirkka-Liisa Konttinen)

being taken over by Riley's at some point. I know Mrs Marriott who lived in 169 Commercial Road. Her son Eddie worked as a snoop for the DHSS, not the most pleasant of jobs but Byker lads were perfect for these difficult jobs as they had any amount of cheek if there was any trouble. He didn't draw attention to what he did. The Raby was called the Grand Cinema in those days, we never understood what was so grand about it! We always called it the

coffin due to its shape, I think everyone did.

Pop and Charlie nearly always had any big jobs that they couldn't do themselves done by Sadlers the builders, who were in Byker Old Village Road – which got to be top Welbeck Road. They were just opposite the reservoir entrance. They also got Josie McFadd to do other joinery work they needed doing. The McFadds were in Byker since early times.

We used to use Morris's chip shop for a

treat but the corner-stone of the street was Chadwick's corner shop. Mr Chadwick was a tolerant and caring person who was quite skilled in making charitable decisions based upon knowing the character he was dealing with. He knew those who were too hard-nosed to trust but would gladly put folks on his slate who he instinctively trusted. He was rarely wrong in his judgements. Today he would be a marketing manager with Boots the Chemist and a lot richer!

All the childcare bits and bobs were down Brinkburn Street, around the library. On one side was the baby clinic, which included the sun ray clinic. On the other side was Wilson's grocer's shop then past an engineering works and you were at Lowry's egg factory.

Olive Lawrence

Street Traders

All our street games could be abandoned at the sound of a bugle from the next street, and the cry which must follow: 'Rags, any ra-ags! Any jam jars, any ra-ags!' At that, the small girl population vanished behind doors and I was left alone listening to the cry coming nearer. The older boys would call out after the rag-man, 'Candy-rock for stocking legs, motor-cars for jam jars.'

Jack Common

Street Sounds

My first recollection is the of the pipe-clay man. 'Cheap stone a penny for three; "barth" brick a penny for two!' he would chant in a sing-song voice. He was obviously a foreigner to these parts with that 'barth'! He also sold salt at 3d a block – like a small doorstep. He would saw off a lump for a penny but the rich would buy the whole block for threepence. It was the duty of the young ones in our large family in turn to scrape a little bath brick on to a plate and clean the family cutlery with a damp cork dipped in the powdered bath brick.

As a kid I knew all their tunes. The fish man would sing 'Caller cod, caller ling' or whatever type of fish he was selling, and this was often accompanied by the appealing cries of a few local cats which followed his cart. The rag man, bag over shoulder, would shout 'Any old rags, bones, boots to sell, any rabbit skins…'

There was the Bombay Tea man. One of these white-coated men would walk up the middle of the lane ringing a hand-bell and chanting 'Bombay, Bombay, given away with half a pound of tea.' Some came round late at night and one was the mussels man. 'Any mussels, fresh mussels.' Then there was the 'Buy-buy-buy-buy-buy crabs' man. He would sing up and down the scale through his cry.

There were other sounds familiar to people of old Byker. One was the grinding wheels of the trams as they screeched around the rails and the clanging of their warning bell. The rattle of mineral water wagons and the clatter of horses' hooves over the cobbled streets. There was the milkman who yodelled his 'Mi-ilk' cry and the lamp-oil man who would ostensibly synchronize his cries of 'lamp-oil' in answer to our own shouts of 'What do you feed your horse on?' Great fun. Too bad for those on night shift but we kids absorbed them all in our own stride.

George Scott

Charles Harrison here celebrates his eighty-fifth birthday at a party in his honour in the Lake District, 21 April 1994.

Everett's

Everett's was a family grocery business that was based at the bottom of Ayton Street on the corner with Raby Street. It was a long way for Granny to walk and instead Pop used to call in there on the way from the Quay and deliver the weekly grocery order. We were loyal to the Everetts as they had been understanding when times weren't so easy. I seem to think our order went in on Monday and was delivered any time around 4 p.m. on Tuesdays. They had a Ford Popular van

with their names on the side. Another Byker business that seemed to thrive in the fifties was that run by Teddy Large. I think they had a stationery business on Byker Bank but they also used to call and collect at regular intervals monies for insurance policies and such like. The Larges seemed to be into all kinds of things. Mrs Large was often the one to call in. She was extremely business-like and dressed very soberly in black. She was in fact black all over from head to foot. She often had a black veil handy and it seemed she could be instantly available for some sombre part of the business she conducted day to day. Teddy Large was well named and fitted his description. The core family business seemed to be in stationery but it's anyone's guess what else they dealt in.

Charlie Harrison

Deliveries

Though milk and bread were front-door deliveries, greengrocery and fish and coal came in the back door. Sometimes for days on end, the children would spend all their time in the back lane, in and out each other's yards, sitting on the steps, or swinging on the lamp-posts. Down here came the Cullercoats fishwives crying 'Caller Herrin!' in that fish's season and otherwise 'Fresh fish, hinny, straight from the sea.' They wore their traditional dress of dark-blue which so well set off the biscuit tan of arm and face, the salt-white hair, and they were like caryatids walking under the great baskets they carried on their heads.

Jack Common

Sandy's Newsagents

The friendly open-all-hours newsagent/sweet shop/corner shop for the streets along the eastern end of St Peter's Road was Sandy's. Sandy Davidson had a thin slick of hair brushed abruptly back. His ruddy face included two very sharp eyes that were partly masked by a set of heavy black framed spectacles. He wore the mandatory sandy-coloured overall – then popular for dealing with the great variety of goods catered for by the corner shop traders. Like so many corner shop owners he was ever present and their hours were 5 a.m. (preparing newspapers) to 8 p.m. This was before the time of the mini-markets and if for some reason he was unexpectedly shut then it would be a minor disaster for those who had run out of tabs or fire lighters or, for the kids, sweets. He was occasionally given relief from front-line duty by the appearance of Belle who, I seem to think, was his sister. My rusty memory seems to think that she died quite suddenly amid much speculation amongst folks as to the cause. I also seem to think that Sandy eloped quite suddenly on a whirlwind romance that was even more talked about. Some years later I heard that he had also died quite suddenly but can't be sure about the date. His shop was in the traditional L-shape. The left hand counter was sweet jars from top to bottom with a mid-way step for the smaller children to stand upon and tender their ha'penny. The right hand counter was more for the adults and had a selection of papers scattered about it. This side was often in use for the paper-boys, who

The horse delivery van of Rington's Tea is still well remembered by today's older people; deliveries ceased around 1957. This scene became the classic icon of this tea that continues to flourish. (NCL)

SANDY'S
95, ST PETERS ROAD

FOR YOUR NEWSPAPERS

PERIODICALS & COMICS

GET YOURS DELIVERED BY OUR

TEAM OF EFFICIENT

NEWSBOYS

ANYWHERE IN BYKER

An advertisement for Sandy's Newsagent's from the Byker Phoenix.

Several members of the Harrison family, originally from Byker, are depicted here at Charles's eighty-third birthday party in 1992. Second from the left is Moyra (now Ingham) and Douglas Harrison (who supplied these pictures) is seated second from the right.

hung about sometimes hours before the papers were due to cadge sweets off Sandy. There was a sort of organized mayhem when you went in for your Sunday morning papers. There were paper boys all around awaiting their call from Sandy for them to come over to collect the papers for their appointed streets. He was mostly assisted by Belle for this important ceremony which included marking them up and skilfully folding them in a certain way which would allow the boy to have the next paper appear after flighting the previous one. He had little time for boys who messed up in the shop. Their services were abruptly curtailed. I can remember seeing a few slope off with their push-bikes between their legs, so to speak, having been sacked. Sandy's was on the Bolam Street/St Peter's Road corner opposite Morris's chip shop.

Charlie Harrison

Wartime

Some Byker kids were the first to be evacuated from Newcastle on 1 September 1939 when over 30,000 went away to Yorkshire and the like. There many more even younger ones soon after, and war was declared on 3 September 1939. Evacuations continued through to the end of 1940 I think. The first air-raid warnings went off on 17 October. The first really big air-raids were early in July 1940 when they got Spillers on the Quay. What a blaze! It was just as well they missed the bridges. In the summer of 1940 we started to get the really big raids with massed planes droning over for what seemed like ages. In Spring 1941 they say that a parachute bomb fell on Shields Road and the area continued to get

blitzed; so much so, that we got a visit from the King and Queen. The worst was to come when in September '41 hundreds of bombs fell on Byker. There were hundreds killed and thousands made homeless in the aftermath. I remember horses being killed down under the Ouseburn. We got another visit by the King and Queen and this time in 1943 they came up Shields Road. By then we had a feeling the tide had turned.

May McClen

CHAPTER 4
Work

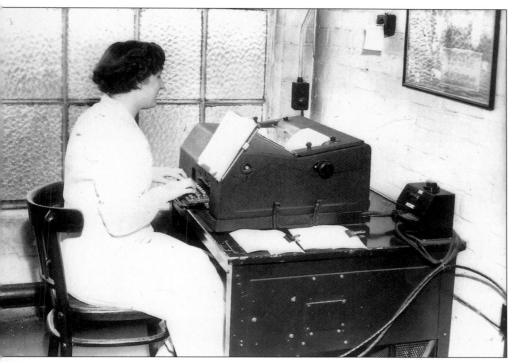

A Byker girl, Fiona Bell, at work at the then new telex installation at Ringtons Tea in Algernon Road, 1954. (NCL)

Bank Holidays

I used to be a signalman in many of the [signal] boxes from Percy Main up to Newcastle itself during the mid to late fifties when I was learning the ropes, so to speak. I'll never forget those holiday weekends – you know – Easter, May bank and especially

August bank holidays when there was a little bit of good weather about.

It started with the Control at Newcastle telling us, maybe the day before, that the bad news was that it looked very like we were in for a bit of fine weather. That was bad 'cause it generally meant that all leave applications were stopped immediately and

A popular destination for everyone on Tyneside was Whitley Bay. This is an outing for the McClen and Groundwater families in 1937.

those on duty in the boxes would have to be prepared to stay on a bit extra like if things got out of hand. The stationmasters all along the coast route stations would get a similar advice and they were told in no uncertain terms that they were expected to be out and about their stations for the majority of the time. There was no quibbling then. We took on these posts and duties with our eyes wide open and knew we would get times likes these so as we took it as a challenge more than any other way, you sees?

Well, come the day and we had battle lines drawn up. The crowds tended to be consistent with the temperature. It would start just as they predicted and as the sun came up there wasn't a cloud to be seen. This was a very bad sign! Next, by about 7.30 in August, say, we would get a steady trickle. These tended to be the older people,

strangely enough. It seemed likely that they were hoping to slope down to the coast before anyone else and maybe get back quicker too. At eight o'clock we would get younger people and the occasional mother and child that might have been up most of the night anyway! But it was after 8.30 that it really began. The Control had a colour system to warn staff of exactly what we needed to throw at them to keep them moving. If the day started hot it was a yellow alert. This meant we kept working a normal day's service but the roster clerks and foreman started to keep an eye out for collaring folks for extra turns of duty. We would put them on standby, see? If the day continued to get hotter we them moved progressively through to orange to finally a red alert. This in effect meant we had every available man Jack at them. Moving upwards of 40,000 people down to the coast and then having to bring them all back again was no mean feat you knows! So by nine o'clock with the sun still climbing we would knew what we were about to receive and those electrics would be running block on block. We would attempt to get the perambulator cars out for about ten-ish when the majority of families with little ones dragging behind might present themselves at Heaton. The stationmasters were clued up and would hold as many prams back as was possible to ease the over-crowding situation. Billy Robertson was a one for this. He had a load of tricks he would try on at Heaton. One was to trick a

load of pram families to go back over to Manors and change there in the belief that it was a quicker run. All these things helped to ease the squeeze see? Them prams in those days were like bloody big chariots. The women sometimes couldn't get the bairns in, as so much stuff was crammed into them for to feed the family. Or it was for nappies – no disposables then, you knows!

By eleven o'clock we would get the final big waves of folks coming mostly up from the bottom end of Byker, cause they weren't any riverside trains for them like. They would be the most awkward cause they would have had to drag the bairns all the

A large fire at Heaton loco sheds in 1918 resulted in this new build of 1938 electric trains which were to become a familiar sight for Byker folk on those hot summer day trips to the coast. In post-war red and white, this train is leaving Newcastle and gives us a glance of a tram. (Courtesy of Alan Thompson)

Byker Junction (or Riverside Junction) stands at the point of the second pole on the left. This picture dates from 1987, when overhead electrification of the main line was advancing through Heaton and Byker.

way up from close on City Road or summit and were already close to the end of their tether. You couldn't get a big pram on the 18. (The No. 18 bus came along City Road and turned up Raby Street to Shields Road and was handy for Heaton Station.)

Walter Anderson

The Return Journey

By about midday it eased enough so as we could get some snap – what Geordies call their bait! We had been out of doors sin' about 4.30, 5-ish – some relief fellers earlier – and this was the first time us railwaymen had got our heads up far enough for to snatch a sandwich. The time flew mind, no

one was complaining, see? Then we had to do it all again in reverse with all the added trouble, but by now us young 'uns knew what to expect and we were primed for it. When I started off being a trainee signalman me old mates down at Normanton used to go on about a busy day cause they'd had twenty-four or so trains through the section in an hour. They said they'd been unable to brew up or read their paper, like. When I came up here to get a promotion I had no idea just how quiet Normanton was because the majority of summer days at Heaton or Manors you never got to sit down once and, if you were lucky enough to have a book lad, you could at least keep the traffic moving and have the luxury of an occasional brew. We would have the problems of tiredness and drunkenness on the way back and you know what that meant! Folks falling out of the doors before the train stopped. I remember some silly sod just walked off the end of the platform instead of going over up the ramp and out. He went off the platform straight onto the lines and simply blew up when he fell on the live rail. Messy!

We would get finished at about 3 p.m. if we had relief. Likely we didn't, or there was no book lad, so the SM [stationmaster] would ask you to stay on for twelve hours. This was common. The normal shift was twelve hours when I first started but became a forty-eight-hour working week soon after. This meant we got one day off a week and worked six shifts of eight hours.

In the early 1960s I got a summer promotion down to Scarborough before coming back to Tyneside as an Inspector in the yards at Heaton.

Author's note: A book lad was a raw recruit who had joined the railway most probably straight from school at fourteen and was starting out on his career. He would start off in a signal box, if he wished to be considered for a career as a signalman, and do nothing other than maintain the train detail entries in the register. Without a book lad, the signalmen were expected to do this themselves but when very busy would often keep a note on scraps of paper and transfer them into the register at the end of

Inside Heaton loco sheds in their final dilapidated condition in 1967. An East Coast express races past a Tyneside electric train (foreground) at the end of its life.

Its a case of 'tempus fugit' as we here witness the last days of 'Heaton for Byker' station in 1975.

Shortly after crossing the Ouseburn Viaduct a LNER engine leaves Byker behind and heads towards Manors in the 1930s. (NELPG)

the shift. An error in the register was considered a serious enough event for it to be attached to the man's history. Several errors could mean demotion to a quieter – and less well paid – box.

Walter Anderson

Domestos Factory

The Domestos factory, just across the other side of the Ouseburn Gut, was independent from its birth in about 1912 up until take-over in 1960. Its products were first marketed as 'Domestos' in about 1930 when under the control of W.A. Handley. It moved over to Lever Bros' control about 1960. The old factory was in use as Mosley's Coachworks for a time and this was originally owned by W.M. Livens & Co. (1920-1930) who were the manufacturers of the sweets sold under the 'College' trade name.

Stan Groundwater

Local Employment

In the fifties the main places our dads worked at were shipyards. There was Hawthorn Leslie's at St Peter's and some went to Walker and Wallsend for the bigger building yards there. The Metal Box Company over at the top of the Shields Road employed some mams and it was close to the Grubb Parsons plant were hundreds worked making the generators. A lot of girls

The Heaton and Walkergate installations supplied much employment for Byker people. This round-the-coast train has left Walkergate station and passes the carriage works on the left, in 1972.

Pickford heavy-lift tractors were a common sight along the industrial belt off Walker Road in 1957. (NCL)

A distant view of Byker, showing the dark mass of Malings Ford Pottery factory with its tower, in 1970. The majority of the houses behind were to be demolished over the next five years.

went to work at Lowry's egg factory or at Rington's Tea place in Algernon Road. Some got work with British Engines down on City Road but they mostly wanted trained engineers and it was hard to get started there. British Electrical Repairs was next to Parsons and employed quite a few.

The Car Sheds were always a good bet for employment if you could drive and had a clean licence. At one point, in the mid-fifties, I bet there were 700 crews and fitting staff seeing to the buses and trolleys then based there.

Some local shops were Jobes and Sandies. There was a medium sized Co-op on Allendale Road.

Nellie Avison

Pottery Works

They say that the Maling's Ford Pottery was the biggest in England when it was expanded into the two factories on each side of the railway sidings. You got in off Walker Road. There was quite an impressive sight greeted you by the Admin Office frontage and the general bulk of the buildings behind towered above the railway here. I think there was also an entrance off Brinkburn Street on the far side. At one time all the sweetie jars were made here and I mean for almost the entire country. I wouldn't like to say how many girls and boys were employed here just churning out thousands of jars day and night. Raw supplies, like flint, came in by rail and it was good business to the old North Eastern Railway. Eventually they must have seen there was more money to be made elsewhere and moved away from jars to high class cutlery, lots of which

would be exported down at the quay – again, more business for the railway. They eventually started producing toilet earthenware and ceramic equipment for the electrical industry which was just starting to boom in the 1900s. Some areas inside were littered with damaged items and staff used to get the pick of any mis-shaped stuff. I suppose even this stuff would be worth a fortune today when you see so many collecting old pottery.

Bob Brennan

Pop's Workshop

My uncle Charlie and Granda 'Pop' were constantly in overalls. Either brown or blue ones depending upon the type of work

1914 workmen's clothes seen in detail on Molineux Street, Byker. (NCL)

they planned to do. Pop used to come up from work on the Quayside already in brown overalls but with a trilby and a blue jacket. I remember his great 'splar' feet almost brushing the pavement before him and his sweeping gait. He arrived from work and expected the worst if I was already there as I frequently would run amok in his workshop out at the back. This was his domain, but what an attraction it was! Especially good were the oiling barrels with press-downs on the top. If I pressed like hell I could just about spray the neighbours' cat (and windows) in oil from these cans. I would run like hell inside when he arrived and laugh uncontrollably as I heard him cursing and tidying up the oily mess. An annoyed 'Pop' had a distinctly attractive appeal and the more he cursed the more I'd bellow with laughter. In a strange way it was making me suffer because he never had any time for me. Oh how I wished he would instruct me with some small carpentry job and trust me, but it was never to happen. Eventually he was to make fewer and fewer journeys down the path to his shed. He was a slightly silly character in my eyes. I used to mimic him blowing his nose and get serious black looks as they struggled not to laugh.

Ken Groundwater

On the Buses

There was always a greasy oily smell from the workmen on the buses and frequently an oil slick on the floor or even the seats.

Another source of work for the area was the Byker Bus Depot of Newcastle Corporation Transport. A trolleybus has been brought out of the shed. (NCL)

During the First World War the shortage of men led to the training of women bus and tram conductors. This party of new recruits are at Byker Car Sheds motor school. A driving mock-up for a tram sits behind. (NCL)

There was always a flat-hatted workman on each bus with a tell-tale oil patch around the centre of his cap where cloth touched Brylcream. In winter the bus was fogged in smoky conviviality and condensation. There was always someone on a Byker bus who was the worse for being well-served and who spoke too loudly. He would go melancholy at the sight of a small child fumble with silver and end up falling off his seat into the aisle by this time wreathed in tears and singing 'Rose Marie'. That was a typical Byker bus.

Stephen Maine

The Byker Grand

I still cry when I remember how they closed the old Byker Grand. To me it was the death of a living thing. Stood on the empty stage, I could hear the past laughter; it was awful. With Emlyn Williams' grim play *Night Must Fall* the curtain came down for the last time in front of a paltry 300-strong audience. A few elderly men and women who had been there for the first performance were present. The Grand closed its doors on August 21st 1954. Producer Patrick Dowling stepped on stage to deliver the final lines with the theatre cat sat at his feet. He said, 'As night must fall on our play, so must it fall on this beautiful theatre and even the cat knows it is the end.'

I first trod these boards at the ripe old age of five. I had been doing a good-luck tour of the dressing-rooms and had accumulated rather too much in food and drink. When I got to go on stage I danced out and was sick down the back of the Principal Boy. She turned around and said 'You little creep.' By the time it came to close I was the manager. I had worked under my father and was paid the princely sum of £10 a week. I had to abide by my father's demands of immaculate dress. It was not nice having to deliver a baby in evening dress but I did, and seven times. I refereed fights between pensioners, was held up at gunpoint and had an elephant do its business all over the orchestra.

In one particular night with *Alfie* playing, we had one birth, two heart-attacks and an epileptic fit. I think it was the heat and excitement that did it. One night I was called to front of the stage to find two old ladies beating each up with their walking sticks. They had been able to afford only one lolly between them and were arguing over whose turn it was to have a lick! On another occasion one little lad was sick all over the orchestra and we had to stop the show for them to change. My father taught me all the tricks like turning the heat up ten minutes before the interval to get them to buy more ices and putting the prettiest usherette in the spotlight at the front. Byker kids could always be relied upon for the unexpected. One night the evil magician in *Aladdin* had had a heart-attack and died. The principal girl came back out for to explain that 'Ebenezer was dead.' From a deathly

silent 2,000 kids, a voice yelled out '...Oh no he isn't.'

David Hinge

Work in the Abattoir

I used to work in the 'killing houses' [abattoirs]. When I first went there we used to kill the cattle with ropes and a hammer. It was a nasty business but work was work. One day there came a chap with a new idea. He had a gun and told me that I'd got to use that to kill the beasts but we had to get his head still first and that meant getting hold of their horns. Man, I divna like that at all. Those beasts were angry; they knew, see, and were dangerous. I'm telling you, they could kill a man – I've seen it happen. So I left them to it – and their humane killer. Mind you, I expect it was better for the beast. The hammer and rope was no good but I left and went into the shipyards.

David Walker

Four Years on the Dole

The thirties were very hard but you knew how to live then. All the people helped each other. I was unemployed for four years and eventually managed to get work as a labourer laying the stones of the Fossway without any machinery at all. I was paid £2 a week and it felt like wealth. All doors along the street used to be open and everyone out standing looking on whilst the kiddies played in those days. We all lived together. When you made bread or scones you also made a load for your

78

neighbours 'cause they would do the same for you.

Albert Jones

Policing Byker

I was a policeman for twenty-six years in Byker. If the men had 2s 6d by the weekend they were millionaires. Yes, they were tough. At the weekend, we coppers used to be out in pairs and there were some rare old fights. Nowadays the men have more sense. They don't pick on coppers so much and life is a lot quieter that way. They were never what you would call a really bad lot, it was just the beer talking. Times were hard and they got a bit over-excited. We knew what they were all up to. We knew their games. For the older men, just after

The red-brick mass of Headlam police station seen from a house-less Corbridge Road, 1973.

Busy Shields Road required police on point duty as seen here at the Brinkburn Street junction in 1970. The Apollo Cinema, near the foot, is also seen in this view, taken from the top near the Blue Bell pub.

the First World War was the worst time for they all had big families and about 30s a week to feed them all on. There were amusements of the kind that needed sentries to look out for coppers. Pitch and toss – called 'hoying' – flourished on Sunday mornings. One Sunday morning entertainment that ceased around about 1950 was short-distance straight-line pigeon racing. To encourage the pigeons to make a sharp take-off firecrackers were tied to their feet. A good deal of scarce money exchanged hands at these Sunday morning sessions. These pastimes were really a link to when Byker was a village and what I suppose you would only call 'peasants' did these similar things.

James Combe

Shell Shocked

He came back from the Somme partly deaf and with a slight loss in vision. All this was due to the gas. You know – the mustard and the like. He got some work with the Corporation on the Quay but it wasn't like real work, it was really stuff that a lad could do but there was still a lot of smaller tasks that he could be trusted with. Because he was known by them before the First World War I think there was a bit of pity that got some of these old boys taken back in. He would be in a sort of trance for long spells and rocked. It was quite difficult at first. He had gone in 1914 as quite normal but quietish and then five years later, this new person returns with old men's complaints that would last

Byker girls including Lorraine Wilson (middle) attend to the packed and finished packets of tea rolling off the Rington's production line in Algernon Road, 1954. (NCL)

A sample of Rington's products in 1954. (NCL)

forever, it seems. Today we might think he was autistic. He could walk past lads fighting something awful or cats and dogs screaming and spitting at each other and he would just keep on going through the middle, walking on as if he was braving a trail through the death and destruction of the trenches carrying his stretchers to the dead and dying. He was a stretcher-bearer with the Northumberlands.

May McClen

An empty Newcastle Brown bottle stands on the chewing gum machine of Young's corner-shop as Byker folk go for their 'tabs' to kick-start the day in 1968.

Religious Friction

Religion, although never any great issue in Byker, nevertheless did form small barriers through the normal misconceptions that adults had about each other and not knowing the truth, and just through ignorance and then passed on down via big-eared kids. St Anthony's was a big Catholic area that revolved around its Catholic school and facilities on Allendale Road. I know that one of its earliest known inhabitants was Dorothy Lawson, 'cause they taught us this much even at our school and how the Lawsons nearly owned Byker, etc. She lived in a time when

A mixed group of four families from Ayton Street and St Peter's Road at Ovingham in 1930.

The same group again at Ovingham, 1930.

Catholic persecution was running high, but somehow she managed to be buried with great honour by the massed ranks from every church in Newcastle.

We always had similar customs, mind. When it came to babies and christenings we were about similar in many respects, though they were more flamboyant with their funerals and I always thought we would be better doing it their way after we saw off Peggie Winship's mother at their church on St Dominic's just off Byker bridge.

Ida Page

Going Out

People only started going out when we got better heated up. That was the start of the leisure industry in my opinion – especially up and down Shields Road and the bingos. You forget there was only pubs open after seven or eight then and it was mostly for men coming back off shifts in factories or such like. They wouldn't want to come straight home – what were they going back to? They were going back to a house full of steam and at least half a dozen naked marauding kids in this process of going to bed. They couldn't face the thought of this after slogging away on their treadmills since about seven or eight that morning. So naturally they would duck out and let things settle before appearing. With central heating it all changed, that, and TV. Our fathers then started to come straight home and that was the difference.

Aggie Stephenson

Charles Harrison and his wife on their wedding day outside St Michael's parish church, Byker.

No Privacy

Then we started courting. Well what a game that was. Where could you go in Byker for a bit of privacy? – nowhere, that's where!

Ernie Neil

Courting in Heaton Park

Everybody knew you wherever you roamed. Even if we went to Heaton Park we would generally bump into Byker lads and lasses. 'Eh, what you doing here, hin?' and 'Is that your lad?' and 'Whatever do ya see in him, lass?'

I think we started the kissing and fumbling stuff, when we discovered that we could stand under some of the back-lane gas lamps unseen. We would be in our own shadow and relatively invisible but that was only any good after autumn. We weren't slow to get courting and I suppose that was down to the fact there wasn't too much to do in Byker when you had passed the street games stage. It was just a natural progression really from playing 'tiggy' and 'squares' if you see what I mean. Mind, I remember five-and six-year-olds in clinches on their doorsteps. I think our parents then were often run so ragged that they didn't always know what we were up to and sometimes things like this happened. I think parents just thought we would play cowboys or soldiers but we were often mimicking what we saw (or heard) our parents doing. In small overcrowded and freezing conditions it wasn't surprising what we saw and understood. We had boys we'd call 'boyfriends' at school, although nowt happened. You went right through school being linked romantically with a certain lad.

Young women's fashions of 1932 are modelled by Winnie and Olive Lawrence.

Some of my friends would call him my 'hubby' and stuff like that but it wasn't until we got the sweats start that you started to look at lads differently and suddenly Byker was a small place and you wanted to get away for some privacy and the like. We could go as I said to the Heaton area and around the park there but these was so many funny types used to hang around the parks. I remember going there when I was about eight – just strayed in – and this red-faced young man said, 'Hey...I've lost one of my children...can you help me find them in these bushes here?' in a sort of cringing and

Byker skyline and St Peter's shoreline in 1968.

apologetic way that I thought wasn't normal. Alarm bells rang inside me even at that age. I had made a half-hearted attempt to help look but gradually got positioned to bolt it. Some of my friends were caught with a similar dodge and ended up racing home after seeing something that really frightened them. So you see Heaton Park wasn't the best of places for privacy if you were courting.

Irene King

Walking for Miles

We would walk for miles – that was courting then. We would never think anything about walking ten miles easily in a day. A typical walk would start with me going from Byker where we lived then, in Raby Street, over to the Coast Road Corner. We would then walk along the Coast Road and through fields to the farm tracks at Benton – behind where the Wills Factory is now. That was a popular parading ground for couples up there. There was sometimes droves of them just going up and down and probably just talking utter rubbish to each other, but it was romantic out of the back lanes and in and around the fields here. Some would find a quiet spot for a canoodle and jump up quick when another couple approached and look all abashed to having been caught. It was gentle stuff compared to today but, oh so romantic and gentle!

Stan Groundwater

Stifling Atmosphere

Well we used to court around these same places, 'cause you wouldn't know anywhere else, 'cause we didn't stray far from Byker and would be frightened to get lost. So we just walked and walked around the edge of Byker. We would link arms and just moon about and stealing the odd kiss in a shop doorway or in a quite lane was such a kick by today's standards but we were just fourteen-ish and the hours would fly by. We would talk and talk a load of nonsense. We would say what we dreamt of being and doing – all mostly daft nonsense. I'd say something like, 'I'm going to London one day soon as me Uncle Tommy has asked me to go down.'

It was mostly to make the lad say, 'Ah, don't go – I love you too much – please don't go.' It was learning about manipulation and artful blackmail for later life, you see? It's something that us girls

learnt pretty quickly. It was survival and growing up and practising being little adults and it was definitely exciting and everything then tingled with anticipation. You didn't want those times to end. My first lad was called Jimmy Cairns. In reality he said something like 'Well, I'm going to sea if you go to London.'

You didn't know, but it was a sparring match. The lads soon cottoned on, mind. We would end up all emotional, almost in each other's arms in tears. It was the intensity of a first deeper relationship and it was a bit scary and at the same time magnetic and there was no escaping and the tears would come around as quickly as the kissing and the smiles went. Byker was no different I suppose from wherever you grew up, but it seemed intense because

A distant view (from Gateshead) of Fuller Road, Burnaby and Graham Street house-ends as they are revealed after the demolition of Dunn Terrace and Salisbury Street in 1970.

there was no hiding place in Byker. We sometimes went as far as Jesmond Dene and one time I remember we got as far as Haddrick's Mill and no money to get a trolley back over to Byker. We loved this new-found freedom and adult talk and adult plans and suddenly Byker was too small for us, and stifling. It was still great to be in the nest but it was also suddenly too much fireside, old people and an island with no escape. It's difficult to explain further than that.

Ida Page

The soot-encrusted rooftops of Mason Street, just below St Michael's parish church high on Byker Hilltop, overlook an ancient Newcastle quayside with the bridges strung out below, 1968.

Race Week

Race week would herald a trek to the Hoppings. Most Byker families then would walk. We would walk up Raby Street, through Shieldfield, along Jesmond Road and onto the Moor. A good time was had by all for about two shillings mainly – in my case – by following the Lord Mayor and obtaining free rides by jumping on anything that he was on! It was great, man!

John Bonner

Music Hall Jokes

'Byker... So good they named it once!' – a gentler example of yet another music-hall style of joke inflicted upon Byker by the comedians upstairs at the Blue Bell's 'come-as-you-please' entertainment nights.

Frankie Johnson

Sunday School

The Revd Baker lived in the vicarage then and he played a big part in putting Byker on the map. He later became a canon and moved to Hexham. One of Byker's first Sunday schools was a hut in Cheviot View, where we kids received religious instructions and sang hymns in the afternoon. In the evenings we watched religious slides through a magic lantern and were told Bible stories. Mischievous boys used to throw tin cans on the corrugated iron roof – they clattered like thunder! If the vicar caught them he brought them inside and made them sit down and listen to the stories. If they were past redemption they were dealt

A Hatful of Rain with Don Murray is advertised as the current running show at the Brinkburn Theatre (the 'Brinkie') in 1957. (NCL)

with by the 'po-liss'. It never took long to reform them – perhaps it was because they used the birch!

Byker was then a safe place to live in, there was never a need to lock doors or windows. Revd Baker raised enough money to build a new three-storey Sunday school. I remember the foundation stone being laid, it was quite a performance. There must have been a thousand children in that building every Sunday.

Louise Toomer

Evening Entertainment

Evenings passed quickly. There was always plenty of household tasks to perform; such as making 'clippie' mats or stippling walls with dish-cloths dipped in distemper and squeezing out surplus paint. They time flew.

We listened to the wireless, visited local cinemas etc. The Raby Cinema, known as the 'Coffin' due to its shape or, in rhyming slang, the Pie and Gravy, was a favourite haunt. Then there was the Brinky (Brinkburn Cinema) and the Impy – the Imperial at Byker Bank. The 'Leccy' was the Electric Cinema on Heaton Road. It was here in these local flea-pits that we watched the Cisco Kid, the Durango Kid, Johnny MacBrown and the rest of our childhood heroes.

John Bonner

Sunday Entertainment

It wasn't all religion. We also had first-class entertainment. There was a cinema on Shields Road called the Sun which held children's matinées every Sunday afternoon.

A typical Newcastle Corporation street cleaner of 1910 with a single horse-power engine. It is passing the Tivoli, once a mission hall, situated on Walker Road, near the old gasworks(NCL)

We got three hours' fun for one penny. We took with us oranges and home-made toffee. Charlie Chaplain made us laugh and cry. We never got tired of watching Mary Pickford being tied to the railway lines. We always warned the engine driver she was there, and assumed he could hear us. We sighed with relief as the train drew up to a halt three feet from her trussed-up body.

We cheered when Tom Mix galloped after a villain. Boys throw their caps in the air and the vandal-proof seats took a rollicking. We could never understand however why the film always snapped just before he caught his man. I've a feeling still that the projectionist liked his fun too. The Sunday school was also our community centre through the week. We didn't have youth clubs, we had friendly societies and boys' brigades. I also have a faint recollection of seeing a Kiltie Band going into Byker parish church and then parading down Headlam Street after the service. Whilst all this was going on the country was supposed to be going through a crisis. If this was a crisis then give me Byker in the 1920s any day! Yes, I think Byker in the '20s had a lesson to teach the whole country and that was money wasn't everything and the best things in life are free.

Louise Toomer

Byker Picture Halls

Can you remember the old Tivoli? It was an old church or mission hall situated on Walker Road near the foot of Raby Street, opposite the old gas works. I can still visualize the old retorts glowing in the darkness of the night. I used to love to swing on the iron gate outside. That, to me then, was an adventure. Can you see seven-year-olds today bothering? I'd fancy I was on the train and stopping at all the stations to the coast. Some years later the Tivoli became a picture hall with 'turns' interspersed between the pictures. I saw Bob Campbell there, the one-legged copper. He sang, as I remember it: 'I'm the one-legged copper with the one-legged trousers'. He would dance around on a single crutch and could miraculously balance himself on the crutch whilst he kicked his one leg into the air. I remember Geordie McCartney, the musician, when he was a tot. He would sit on the back wall of Priory Street – now no more – playing an old German concertina. In later years he could knock a tune out on almost anything. Among the other picture halls in Byker was one called the Sun. It was on Byker Hill. The audience sat on forms and a piano played 'mood' music. Admission was 4d or 6d. Even before the Brinkie (Brinkburn) was built, a marquee stood on the same site and was owned by the Cottrill family who did underwater feats in a tank. The audience were shown films which together with the aquatic feats of the Cottrill girls. It lasted about twenty, thirty minutes and was considered then to be quite good value for an admission fee of 2d. Then there was the Grand Theatre where we boys could enjoy a twice nightly show of variety in the 'gods' for 2d.

'Early doors this way,' the uniformed doorman would shout, allowing the Byker elite to choose the best seats for a few coppers extra while the less affluent ones would have to risk a later shout of 'House full!' A critical audience would show its appreciation of the better turns vociferously or proffer raspberries to the 'mugs'. Many good artists performed there for what some modern entertainers would call 'small change'.

When funds were low – and remember that 6d was a fortune in the 1920s – we had other means of entertainment like tying

Molineux Street back lane, looking north-east, in 1914. The advertisements include promotions for the Scala Electric Theatre and Heaton Electric Palace. The very large Post Office masts in two locations are curiosities not found elsewhere at this time in Byker. (NCL)

Looking south along Heaton Road in 1912. On the right is the entrance to the station and, beyond, is the Electric Palace which vied with Shields Road amenities for the custom of Byker folk. (NCL)

neighbouring doors together with string or such other pranks. That was as near to vandalism as we got then.

George Scott

A Bit of Broon

The Snug in these locals is like a free club for us – they ask no admission fee here, beyond the price of a glass. I drink nowt else but Broon. I won't even look at these frothy visiting ales, no point; I'm happiest with me Broon! Most that comes in here are Broon drinkers and we view very suspiciously the lager drinking brigade – not real men. There are loads of pubs throughout Byker like this one and you'll find the true Byker lads have a passion for Broon. Womenfolk like the Broon as well... Our lass put the young 'un asleep many time by the application of a little bit broon – does no harm, like. There used to be a few terrace pubs along here where folk hardly need step out their door to get in – you could step in and fall out and be yerm [home]! The young 'uns like vodka but wes old 'uns like our Broon and we'll stay that way till we drop.

There some pubs along Shields Road bottom end where they made changes but in most pubs round here they hardly changed in fifty year.

Joe Simpson

The RAOB

Arthur Nattrass was the Secretary of the RAOB (Royal Antediluvian Order of Buffaloes) Club and Institute on Heaton Road, Byker, in May 1965.

We are a very progressive club. In 1950 our takings were £9,800 and in 1964 we took £60,000. We have a progressive committee. We have already bought up the premises on each side of the club for expansion and are always trying to improve things. We are getting the decorators in soon. The loans for the extensions are paid for by loans from the Newcastle Brewery and the club's bank and we have paid most of the bank loan off already. We now have 945 members and a large waiting list. We couldn't take on any new members last year – that's how popular this club now is. We don't lose any members either. We have big footballing connections at this club and that might be part of the attraction for the male members. Our own footie team is top of the North-East Sunday League in its first season of trying so we're a bit proud of that. We have Charlie Crowe's dad come in here regular. (His son, also Charlie Crowe, was once a great crowd-pleaser at St James's Park.) We also get quite a few talent scouts congregate in here to swap notes about young talent in the area. Over there now at that table is Jack Hixon and George Murray. They are both talent scouts for Burnley. We also have a lot of staff. We need to with almost 1,000 people in here for the biggest events.

For over two years now our Steward and Stewardess have been Joe and Gladys Gibson and they have command of twenty-two

In this view of the eastern section of Shields Road on 11 June 1974, the traffic is already beginning to build up towards today's proportions. The white-painted Blue Bell pub is prominent. (NCL)

barmen, waitresses and doormen. Our vice-chairman is Sid Field. We are next planning to convert the men's lounge into mock Tudor decor. At the moment it's only used for storing chairs when we have dancing in the concert room. Currently our oldest member is sixty-eight-year-old Arthur Jones. He has been a member twenty-three years and he told me he approves of the club's new look. Arthur was a war hero, he was awarded the Military Medal and Bar in the First World War.

Arthur Nattrass

Couldn't Afford a Pint

We all know each other and that's why its like a club at the bottom of the street. I can remember the days about thirty-forty years ago when I couldn't afford a pint, not once a week. I'm seventy-two now. I've seen me so fed up on a Saturday neet that I'd stand on a corner just hoping someone would come along that I knew with a few coppers to spare. See, work was bad back then. In those days these places meant everything. It provided the escape we needed in those bad times. Byker just wouldn't be the same without its fifty or so pubs.

They're planning to bulldoze down these streets – I just hope they leave the pubs standing! Certain things never change and if our lass forgets to wake me for opening time she'd get it. She knows how important it is to me!

Joe Simpson

A night out on 29 October 1975 for members of the Middle Club. (Courtesy of the Byker Phoenix)

Byker's Clubs

This is an extract from Ward's Directory of 1926 listing the clubs, institutes and societies available to Byker's residents at that time.

Walker and Byker Industrial Mechanics' Institute, Church Street.

British Legion Club & Institute Ltd, (Byker and Heaton) 2 Stephen Street.

Byker & Heaton Conservative Working Men's Club, 2 Wilfred Street.

Byker & Heaton Union Ltd, 290 Shields Road.

Byker & St Peter's Working Men's Social Club, 171 Raby Street.
[This was known as the 'Middle Club'.]

St Peter's Social Club, of Raby Street.
[It was originally known as the 'Bottom Club'; its replacement now stands in Bolam Way.]

Byker Reservoir

Byker Reservoir was used by Newcastle & Gateshead Gun Club in the late 1960s, run by Brian Laverick. The club practised shooting along the length of a disused reservoir. They had a heavily secured shed at one end for storing (mainly) .22 single-bore rifles.

Ken Groundwater

Black's Regal

Black's Regal opened on 3 September 1934 at the top of Shields Road, to the left. The first showing was *Fashions of 1934*. It seated 1,120 in the stalls and 525 in the circle. In 1955 it became part of the Odeon group and was renamed that. It closed as a cinema in 1972 and was demolished completely in 1986 or 1987. There were another two cinemas with the same name and all built in the north-east by Alfred Black (Sunderland (1932) and Gateshead in 1937).

Stan Groundwater

Byker Pubs

The Blue Bell stood at top (in the 'V') of Shields Road and Union Road. It stood on the site of the long-standing home of the once well remembered Lawson family. Do you recall that the Glendale, in Potts Street, was voted Pub of the Year in 1982, when under the management of that charming landlady Mrs Audrey Nicholson? The New

"AYE GEORDIE - ME AND WOR LASS IS BEEN MARRIED THORTY YEARS AND WA STILL IN LOVE.
SHE LOVES THE BINGO AND I LOVE THE BOTTOM CLUB!"

This amusing advertisement used to grace the wall by Byker Bridge on the way into the City. It is seen here in 1970. (EC)

Hawk Inn, Byker Bank, was always popular with the City Road lads that I knew. They reckon it was rebuilt in 1880 after the first the (Old) Hawk just about fell down from the fighting and antics in them barbaric times! But the most famous of all had to be Jocker Wood of the Masons Arms. He won all five events – Quoits, Pigeon Flying, Bagatelle, Cycling and Golf – way back when men were men and a Byker pub rarely saw a woman – except for the barmaid.

George Scott

Miscellany of Pubs

In 1975, the Plough Inn shut all day Wednesday due to the recession and poor business.

The Viaduct Hotel was one of the toughest in the Newcastle area. In 1975 it went onto a six-day week. It was then run by 'Ginger Roberts', actually George Robertson, who was once a very good boxer. He had been the Northern Area Welterweight Champion.

I also remember the old pentagon-shaped public conveniences that where in the middle of the road at the top of Shields Road.

Tommy Boyd

Formal Viewing

Sunday tea-time was a big social event when you had a girlfriend. It was the formal viewing of her, you see. My mother said I could invite Olive over for next Sunday and know this was her big test. She got on well with Violet straight away and made her laugh. They got on well forever after this good start. Olive always used to make my mother laugh but there was nothing she could do to make my father like her. He could hardly speak to her much ever. They sort of put up with each thereafter but he was a funny, strange man.

Stan Groundwater

Cowboy Films

It was smashing in Raby Street when you knew who yer neighbours were. They were all canny and dead good to you. We would just gan into each other's hooses for a natter – it was smashing then. A treat was better than it is today; I mean it was hard worked for, you knows. We bairns were got out of the way on Saturday mornings. It was the big treat of the week. We would all meet up with our mates as we went along the road towards the Raby [the Raby Cinema]. We would pack inside somehow – there must have been about 400 inside, no kiddin'. It was generally a cowboy film and me favourites were Roy Rogers. The noise was terrible. We would all shout out at the bad 'uns and give instructions to the good 'uns and the like. It was too much for some of them and bigger girls kept coming round to see if the little 'uns weren't too frightened at the noise an all. Some burst into tears as soon as the lights went out and were taken care of by the big lasses.

Don't know how it worked but on coming out we were given a goody bag. There was a

From left to right, Walter Fell, Evelyn Marriott, Olive Lawrence and Eddie Marriott at South Shields in 1934.

Jeffrey Atkinson (left), Ken Groundwater and Kenneth Bird in Ayton Street in 1956.

mixture of bullets [sweets] inside and always a nice new shiny sixpence, which was a lot then for us kids. We would go straight to one of two sweet shops and the blighter was spent before our mams could 'take care of it' for us!

Frankie Johnson

Meeting in the Cinema

The cinema got to be everything to us when we reached a certain age and had pals. We didn't stray much out of Byker then. The cinemas along Shields Road/Heaton Road were the farthest we got. I met Olive at a party for Walter Fell. His sister somehow

knew Olive and there she was. I was three years younger and she seemed unapproachable but I was daft on her and kept bothering her. I got told to run along and see me mam and things like that but somehow she must have seen something there and eventually said, 'All right, I'll see you for a walk out next Sunday.' I said, 'Come up to see my Aunty Margaret,' and she did. I was quite quiet around her but she stuck with me ever afterwards apart from a bit of trouble with her family. They lived at Heaton, next to the Coast Road Corner. No. 15 Coast Road in fact – it's still there although the big roundabout's gone, replaced with a dive-under now. Her family

The author's father doing an impression of his hero James Cagney outside 201, Ayton Street, in 1937.

she had five sisters) took one look at me and said, 'Olive, you don't want to get involved in anyone from Byker' – below her, see? – and then they said I was a little Jew boy – I think 'cause of my dark complexion.

Stan Groundwater

Byker Grand

Byker Grand opened on 27 July 1890. In 1936 a box seat cost 2s 4d and one in the gallery was 4d. Bobby Thompson – 'the little waster' – got his first chance here. Charlie Chaplin appeared here in 1924. It closed in August 1954. It was still for sale in September 1955 (at £11,000) and was ultimately demolished a couple of years later.

Willie Harle

Boys' Brigade HQ

The building that was formerly the vicarage of St Michael's church is now David Grieve House. About 1963-4 it passed to the Boys' Brigade who used it as the HQ for the Newcastle Division Battalion and named it after Dr David Grieve who did so much for the BB and who died in January 1964. A sad sight will greet ex-BB members today [November 2000] as the house is derelict, boarded over with a large 'For Sale' sign flapping against it and few takers for the price, bearing in mind its location.

Stan Groundwater

Tanner Hops in the Thirties

For us then Shields Road was the glittering Broadway in the lives of us young masters.

The Marriott and Groundwater 'Al Capone' contest appears to be taking place on the south pier at South Shields in 1935.

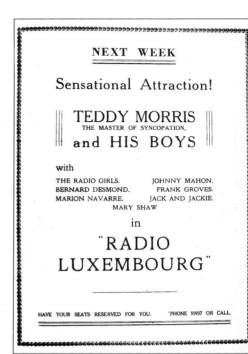

Four playbills from the Byker Grand Theatre. (NCL)

FOR PATRONS' INFORMATION

TIMES - - - - - - Twice Nightly, 6-30 and 8-45 p.m.
BOOKING OFFICE HOURS - - - - 10 a.m. until 9 p.m.
'PHONE NUMBER - - - 55934.

PRICES:
Orchestra Stalls and Dress Circle - -	1/3
Stalls and Circle - - -	1/-
(The above Reserved Free of Charge.)	
Pit Stalls - - - - -	9d.
Gallery - - - - -	4d.
Children - - - 8d., 6d. and 5d.	
Box Seats - - - - -	2/4

NO CHARGE FOR BOOKING.　　　500 Circle and Stalls seats reservable at 1/-

Cars may be parked (with lights) in Wilfred Street. An attendant is in charge but no responsibility can be accepted for theft or damage.

Patrons anticipating 'phone calls or urgent messages are requested to leave their seats numbers at the Box Office or with any attendant.

The theatre is fully licensed and the Circle, Stalls and Gallery Buffets are open from 6 p.m. until 10 p.m.

Chocolates and Cigarettes are obtainable from the Attendants and in the Buffets.

Smoking is permitted. Patrons are requested to deposit cigarette and cigar ends in the ash trays provided.

In case of fire on the stage the fireproof curtain will be lowered immediately to render the auditorium safe. Adequate exits are provided in each part of the house and in case of emergency the theatre can be cleared in two minutes.

A limited number of advertisements can be accepted for this programme. For terms apply to the Manager.

SABEY & BEST, NEWCASTLE-ON-TYNE.

Week Commencing Monday, April 27th, 1936.

PROGRAMME

ELDON PRODUCTIONS LIMITED,
present

The Charles Denville Famous Players
IN

"COMMON CLAY"

CAST:
Samuel Fielding	ALFRED FARRELL
Richard Fraser	CHARLES DENVILLE
Hugh	JOHN MORGAN
Archie Coburn	WALTER LEYBOURNE
Gus Blinder	FRANK LISTER
Abel Yales	JOHN HADDLETON
Edwards	ARTHUR C. CROSBY
Patrolman Kelly	FRANK TWITCHEN
Judge	FRED GRANVILLE
Martha Nelson	DOROTHY HILDEBRANDE
Mrs. Fielding	CHRISTINE BENNETT
Gwen Pacey	LILY DENVILLE
Helen Nelson	VERA FRENCH

THE ITALIA SIX TROUPE OF DANCERS, GUESTS, POLICE, USHERS, &c.

Extra Ladies and Gentlemen by courtesy of The Miniature Theatre and Raymond Woolf, Esq.

SYNOPSIS OF SCENERY :
Scene 1	LIVING ROOM AT THE NELSON'S HOME
Scene 2	NEAR THE PARK
Scene 3	BLINDER'S NIGHT CLUB
Scene 4	HOME OF THE FRASERS
Scene 5	JUDGE FIELDING'S CHAMBERS
Scene 6	THE COURT
Scene 7	CORRIDOR IN THE FRASER'S HOME
Scene 8	DRAWING ROOM AT THE FRASERS'

THE KING.

David Anderson as Cinderella in the Byker Community Centre production of February 1975.
(Courtesy of Sirkka-Liisa Konttinen)

We wore dark-blue trilby hats, dark-blue overcoats tight at the waist, and shoulders well padded – the American gangster look. I recall the 'tanner' hops. One night it would be at the Byker Parish, another evening we would dance, laugh and flirt at the 'happy hour' in the room above the 'Chillie' [Chillingham Hotel], where our sixpence admission fee would include a supper of meat pie and tea. Another hop was at a place near Millers Road and music was provided by accordion plus drums. Our big nights were at the Heaton Assembly Rooms with good old Henner Huspith's band. All the local firms went there for their staff dances. Beavan's, Parrish, Hodgkins' Metal Co. and Rington's – and I usually managed to get tickets. Then there were the many billiard halls of those days. There was one below the street level at the Heaton Assembly Rooms, one in a shanty on Union Road, another about opposite the Raby Hotel. Those days and nights were ended when a little man in Germany plunged the world into war. No more tutti-frutti at Mark Toney's or fish and chips at Barry's. Shields Road became blacked out and the Apollo Cinema received a direct hit. Things certainly changed after the war. The folks in Byker are better dressed than they were in the thirties, with more to eat, but the true spirit of Byker is called neighbourliness and may that spirit never be bulldozed away!

Jimmy Walker

Churches

St Lawrence's iron mission church was almost opposite the 'bottom club'. In about 1908 it was replaced by the new brick church at the foot of St Peter's Road. The old 'iron church' – as it was called – became used as the church hall and was later called 'the shack' by generations of Byker boys who passed this way. It was closed in 1979 and was merged with St Michael's parish church. In 1983 it was finally demolished. The houses of Fenning Place now stand on the site. I have happy memories of the rough and tumble games we earnestly looked forward to. We enjoyed this 'organized' madness more than just flying loose about Byker for some reason. I suppose it was because we were adult supervised and wanted – like most Byker lads – to please so much that we would run ourselves ragged.

Stan Groundwater

St Michael's Church Vicars

Former vicars at St Michael's church include, from 1953 to 1962, R.F. Grist, and before him was the Revd W. Usher (1947-1953). The most well remembered was Revd (eventually Canon) Baker, from 1925 to 1938. The centenary of the church was on 12 March 1962.

Also there was Leighton Primitive Methodist Chapel. The Presbyterian Church of England church was in Gordon Road and the date on its foundation stone was 22 March 1902. St Silas' was built in 1886 and still exists in 2000, and is now the oldest operational church in the area.

Stan Groundwater

Flower Shows

My grandfather and Uncle Charlie were daft over dahlias and chrysanthemums. I

St Lawrence's church between Till Street and St Peter's Road in 1902. (NCL)

remember them taking me to the City Hall for a show. They had to collect these green standard type showing vases. They spent ages on their presentations and ended up getting nothing. I remember they had their blooms in large paper bags for ages to stop pests (like me!) and damp and rain getting to them and spoiling them before show-time.

Ken Groundwater

The New Hawk Inn

The New Hawk Inn was built around 1881 to replace the old Hawk Inn on the opposite side of the street. The latter became a rag shop of Freddie Shepherd. On the other corner of Ford Street once stood the Talbot Inn – next to Jeannie Raine's pie and stotty shop. In 1927 Bob Gray and family moved into the Hawk. Bob was a champion sculler on the Tyne and in his later years was the referee for the river races from Hawthorn Leslie up to Scotswood. The next manager at the Hawk was Seaman Watson, the most famous boxer Byker ever produced. He converted the upstairs meeting room into a gym and would spar with other local boxers in preparation for his world title fight in the New York. When he went to America to fight 'the Kid' he was thought not to be good enough and had to box Barber first before he got a crack at the champ and the title.

When 'Seaman' left the Hawk in 1932 he ran the Wolsington Hotel and later the

An outing by bus in 1953, Coronation year. Centre stage in this view is Margaret Whaley (née Groundwater) and her son Donald is to her left. To his left is Maude Whaley.

Gun, in Scotswood. He left on the Sunday night and handed over £18 for a week's takings to the next manager, Archibald Brown. From then on the Hawk became known as Dyer Brown's Bar. Dyer was the most respected and well-liked manager of all time at the Hawk. His wage in 1932 was £2 10s a week and from this he had to maintain the pub. In those days whisky was 12s 6d a bottle and beer was 5d a pint. Wilkinson's mild was 4d, Nut Brown Ale was 5d a bottle and the stronger BPA special was 8d a pint. This was known as 'Baden Powell's Army' to many.

Apart from the local people of Byker Bank, dockers and Irish labourers began to use the Hawk and many drank on 'tick' and settled their debts to Dyer on pay day. If anyone failed to pay up then Dyer and his two sons would go into Melton's Lodging House and turn the beds over until they found the man. He usually paid up or was in for a beating.

During the night shift in winter, Anderson from the nearby glassworks would call at the Hawk around three o'clock in the morning for the two pails of beer set aside for him for to quench the thirsts from the hot furnaces. Dyer would also rise from his bed in the early hours and make up flasks of hot oxo with rum and then take them down to the docks where his regular customers were working during the winter nights. Originally a blacksmith's striker in the shipyards, Dyer first managed Jocker Wood's bar in Quality Row, the Masons Arms. He and Jocker were rival quoit players and the rivalry ended when Dyer beat Jocker on the quoit pitch attached to the Duke of York Pub in Maling Street. Dyer thus became the champion, though it was never official. His son Steve Brown joined the Navy in 1940 and served on the Tyne-built destroyer HMS *Mendip*. Steve saw service in North East coast convoy duty from Sheerness and Rosyth, and with Middle East troop ships to Gibraltar and Malta. He married while on leave and lived in the Hawk for a time until he moved to Burnaby Street.

Tommy Burn

Funeral Ceremonies

There was a communal wash-house and our mothers would take turns in all weathers. We played in the Burn and occasionally we would venture into the 'cully' and walk to the other end in total darkness, all of us holding hands. When we got to the other end we would walk back again. My most vivid memory is of funerals. Oh, how Byker people loved them! The great big horses and the carriages – they filled the whole street. I can remember one day when there were two on one day. The second death was the lady who had just 'laid out' the first! Imagine all the pomp and ceremony in such a small street. One lady was self-appointed to bring out a tray of whiskies, wearing a clean white apron. She would give this to the driver up on his seat, 'a drink to keep the cold out'. Though even on hot days they got their drink. Now, they cannot put them away quickly enough. Gone are the days of ham teas and whisky. Between the bridges was the Shields kipper house where we used to get a bundle of broken kippers for a copper –

they were smashing. Then there was Faith's Furniture factory where about one in every ten Byker girls worked at some point. There was the paint factory where we got the yellow ochre for the doorstep and the abattoir not many yards away. There was also a sail-loft factory and the only other work I can think of was the tripe shop. My family moved out of the Burn in 1967.

Mona Milor

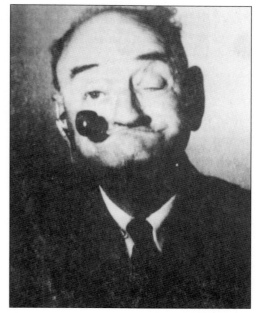

George McCartney of 83 Bolam Street was well known to people as a bit of a character. His gurning or impressions of Popeye entertained many over the years! (Courtesy of the Byker Phoenix)

CHAPTER 6

Changing Byker

A 1980 view of the top of Ayton Street that somehow survived the Byker Redevelopment. On the right sits the dark red-brick mass of Bolam Street Schools.

Parochial Tightness

Attached to Byker's east end is Walker but along the riverside there is a slight blurring of territory as Bird's Nest and Pottery bank form indistinct boundaries within Walker and Byker itself. There has always been quite a bit of movement to and fro between these areas whereas to step outside these areas completely would have been tantamount to going on the moon – such was the parochial tightness of these riverbank communities at least, that what was what I always thought.

Stan Groundwater

The Velvet City

I said I wouldn't leave, and then when I had to go, I said I wouldn't stay a week and here I am – still here thirty years on. I didn't like the surroundings a bit but I've gradually become used to life here and don't suppose I shall move anywhere else now. I loved it down old St Peter's. It was called the 'Velvet City' by those that lived there. There was always something happening there, accordion players in the streets, things like that. It was marvellous.

Honor Dodgson

What was Dents Hole grew into the location of Hawthorn-Leslie's engineering site hard on the river and adjacent to the 'Velvet City'. The area is seen here in 1970. It has since been cleared for the Marina development.

Old St Peter's Village

Demolished nearly seventy years ago, in the 1930s, only a handful of people remain in 2000 who once lived in the old St Peter's Village. No evidence remains of the place today. Maurice Rotheroe, however, captured some memories in 1960 of those who once did live there and has graciously allowed me to reproduce some of their anecdotes. Maurice says that they were building Evistones Gardens at about the time the old village went and a fair proportion of the villagers went into homes there. This is what some had to say.

Electric Dangers

I had six children when I came to the Gardens and had another two here. The big danger in moving was the river and the electric railway. It was a very big worry to me when the children were young. Several people have been drowned in the river here and children electrocuted on the live rail.

Mary Dodgson

Drowning Tragedy

Two years after moving from the old village into the Gardens my eighteen-year-old son was learning to swim in the river when he was drowned. Another boy went in to save him, and he was drowned too. I shall never forget that tragedy. The whole of Evistones Gardens went down to the river to help. There were what looked liked hundreds of folk down there but what could they do? Life has to go on and we got over it eventually. This street is very friendly and

I've got some good neighbours. My son James has painted every house in the street; he works for Newcastle Corporation as a painter.

Mary Sanderson

Rats

Despite the very sociable atmosphere of the old Velvet City the houses were falling to pieces and were rat infested. I remember taking part in street marches in the 1920s for new homes, so I can't say I was sad to leave.

Mary Brereton

Two Wars' Service

I've spent many years in and out of Newcastle. I joined the Women's Auxiliary Army Corps in the First World War and reached the rank of sergeant-major and served in France. I joined up again in the last war and became a corporal. I was one of the first ATS to be sent to Egypt.

Violet Wilkinson

Children's Careers

I was born in Yarmouth Town but came to Newcastle as a child. My husband Fred and I have lived in the Gardens seventeen years. I have had six children and they all have a variety of jobs. My eldest daughter, Mrs Annie Ireland, is a Salvation Army Officer. Frederick was a schoolteacher until illness prevented him carrying on. Another son is a bus driver, a third is a fitter. My daughter Dorothy is a senior shop assistant and my youngest daughter Cynthia is a telephonist. They say variety is the spice of life!

Gladys Page

St Peter's Finale

Around 1880 St Peter's was made up of a collection of short streets to the west of Rose House culminating in a sanatorium and manure works. At first the T.W. Smith shipbuilding site dominated the riverside but later became Hawthorn Leslie's much-expanded manufactory. On each side were areas loosely known as Dents Hole and the 'Mush' (Mushroom) that was itself once peppered with small boat-building yards and staiths, and their associated pubs. The surrounding area changed to accommodate the railway early in the twentieth century. Today the old railway route is a walkway running from Walker to the eastern edge of the plush new St Peter's Marina mews with vessel moorings. The old bone-yard that cast its distinctive 'perfume' over Byker on hot days has thankfully been another casualty of time in this area. The new St Peter's developers once cast an envious eye upon the allotment space below Harbottle Park and, no doubt with time, these also will tumble in the face of corporate wealth as river views with moorings mimic the London riverside regeneration.

St Peter's Marina

This area has come from being the foulest stinking hole in Byker – as the ironically named 'Velvet City' – into being the plushest in the North East (if not the North). But it still has the hand of old Byker influence over it as the new wealthy residents discovered, in 1994, when the

The highest street in Byker was Cheviot View. In this 1969 photograph, the tower of Headlam Street police station can also be seen.

This scene along Albion Row's back lanes was photographed on 4 February 1969, months before they would be lost forever. (NCL)

Ralph Erskine's dream for Byker materialized in 1975 with a successful integration of styles 'by the people for the people'. (NCL)

Marina was becoming established. It was noticed by some residents that Freddie Shepherd's scrap-yard was slightly 'pongy' and a bit of an eye-sore. As Freddie told the press 'I was here first and have in fact been here with my business over thirty years now.' We are pleased to report that an amicable arrangement was eventually achieved.

Ken Groundwater

Redevelopment

Before the redevelopment began there were over 17,000 people tightly packed into these Tyneside flats, which were often overcrowded and lacking in basic amenities. Some parts had already been condemned for some time and others were brought into the slum clearance programme of 1960. By 1963, the whole of Byker was scheduled for redevelopment, enveloped in the Wilfred Burns plan to demolish a quarter of the city's entire housing stock by 1983. What makes Byker special is that in 1968 the council decided to respond to local demands and to acknowledge that here was a cohesive community which should be sensitively conserved, rather than sacrificed in a dash to create a kind of Venice of the north. The council decided to make a break from the familiar numbers game and to emphasis instead redevelopment based on the existing community. The appointment of Ralph Erskine, as architect, symbolized the break with tradition.

At the start of demolition the population had declined by 75 per cent and after the decision in 1968 to retain the community it has fallen by 64 per cent. Erskine had proposed to move over 9,000 people in the scheme and the intention was that most of the people remaining in Byker at February 1970 would be given the chance to remain. By January 1979 the population was only 4,400 and there were 1,000 dwellings to be built, but only fifty old houses to be demolished. This meant that 40 per cent of the dwellings would be built after the removal of the people who had originally expected to move in. As a result of this it becomes clear that only slightly more than 50 per cent of the new units went to Byker people and that at least 5,000 households left the area permanently whilst the transition was ongoing. One is left to speculate as to what might have happened had the policy not been to retain the community.

Peter Malpass

Researching Byker

The following section is reproduced by courtesy of Sirkka-Liisa Konttinen, a Finnish woman who lived and worked in Byker from the 1960s. As a background to her comments, she offers the following statistics from a Durham University research project on Tyneside from the mid-sixties:

68% of residents continue to live in Byker after marriage
40% have more than two relatives nearby.
40% see at least one relative every day
46% shop only in the Byker area
45% shop mainly on Shields Road
77% wanted to be re-housed in Byker.

Sirkka's Background

I came to live in Byker at the start of the redevelopment and stayed until I was bulldozed out of Janet Street in 1976. During the years from 1970 the old way of life held a very special attraction to me. The community was still going strong in its run-down setting. My street was made up of a handful of old Byker families, with grandparents, uncles, cousins and newly-wed daughters living doors from each other. The daughter, mother and grandmother would meet in the pub at the bottom of the street for a chat and a sing-song. The father and son raced pigeons down on the railway embankment. The second-hand shops flourished in Raby Street then, there was still room for initiative and imagination. The old people, the children and the loners like 'Dummy' and 'Darkie' were important and functioning ingredients of the community, all part of an intricate pattern of mutual need and care and much based on unquestioned, 'old-fashioned' humanistic values. The interesting debate is whether (and for how long) their way of life would have continued if left undisturbed.

For me, in the late 1960s, the vision began from the hill, sweeping down along the steep cobbled streets with row upon row of terraced flats, into the town, over the river and the bridges and beyond. The streets of Byker, serene in the morning sun with smoking chimney pots, offered me no paradise; but I was looking for a home.

Walking down Janet Street on that soft Saturday in the late autumn, I was put under a spell. That spell was to last for ten years; after which there were no women to stand in the doorways and no dogs to doze on the pavements, and no streets to run down the steep hill.

Many Byker men made their way each day along the eastern part of Shields Road towards this heavy engineering zone with Grubb Parsons at its centre. Above is the older part of the works, while the 1955 extension is seen in 1957, below. (NCL)

Byker Memories

Unhurried Saturday shoppers in Raby Street. Bursts of merriment outside the grocer's shop and in the butcher's queue. The baker's tray cooling off by the door, besides the bacon and the buns. Frankie Laine reaching out to a passing audience from a wind-up gramophone outside Henry's Square Deal Store: 'East is East and West is West', etc., then: 'Love is a Golden Ring…'

Three weeks later I was pushing around my first proud possession in my own little upstairs flat in Mason Street. Once satisfied I had found it a place, I wound it up, threw open its volume-control doors, and let loose 'Sparrow in the Treetop' to bounce around the tiny room, and to welcome me home.

Traditional bus routes were disrupted by the redevelopment. Here in 1973 the No. 12 takes to Raby Street for a short distance.

The first night I sat alone in the Hare and Hounds I was taken under the collective wing. The drinks arrived with but a smile and a nod from an assortment of kindly faces round the room. Mrs Dunn tucked me to her bosom 'That man of yours, does he belt you?' was one of the first questions. 'You come and tell me – old Mrs Dunn, number seventeen – if he so much as lays a finger on you, hinny, and I shall see to him.'

After a week I saw her in the street again. She linked my arm, winked and steered me to the pawnshop. 'He's a fine young man, your man,' she beamed at me. 'Bless you both,' and she pressed a piece of folded paper into my hand, with a wedding ring inside. I wore that ring, for her, till it dropped off my finger, and speeding down the pavement finally bounced out of sight, and out of my life.

The Start of Research

I had a cat; he vanished one day, like all the other cats in the street, and I was united with the rest of the street in shameless speculation. I then set up a portrait studio in an empty hairdressing salon in Raby Street, and invited passers-by in for to have their photos took. I moved on to photograph families at home. It grew to be my ambition to photograph every household in my street.

I received a mixed response. 'I'm sorry, pet, but I've never had a photo took of me in all me life. It's no good now, hinny, I'm past it now.' And; 'Well, hinny, I've got hundreds of pictures, I don't need another one took. Come and see for yersel'; got so many I don't know what to do…' Or: 'Me husband works neets. No, I can't be bothered, pet, but thanks all the same.'

Billy Thompson, one of Byker's window-cleaners, in Mason Street, 1975. (Courtesy of Sirkka-Liisa Konttinen)

I got a 'yes' from half the households, and half of those had better things to do when I turned up with the equipment. But I did manage to capture a fine series of mantelpiece displays, which were always promptly made available for my documentation. Lovingly arranged, in perfect symmetry, they were meant for the admiring visitor.

Sirkka's work in Byker became known, accepted and assisted, and her collection of photographs, poems, reminiscences and memories began to grow.

Willie and his Mouth Organ

I first met Willie playing a mouth organ at a street wedding. He had popped the wee instrument into his mouth, to free his hands for the spoons, and he danced like a nimble circus bear. He later polished off his act by including a hat trick and an anecdote or two, and he often entertained all day in Isaac's second hand shop. As a young man he worked in the Royal Victoria Infirmary, and in a boiler room explosion lost acres of skin. He was dipped in ether, rolled into cotton wool and left to hang on, whereby he survived to tell one tall story after another. He used to turn up in my studio with a plastic parrot, and a fiddle with Guarnedi rubber-stamped on the inside – a fine instrument, which he couldn't play but loved to be photographed with it. He was a champion draughts player: and was capable of standing in an immaculately frozen pose for the quarter of an hour at a time, as he frequently failed to plug in his hearing aid for further instructions.

The Hare and Hounds

The Hare and Hounds' at the bottom of Janet Street became my local. Mothers, daughters and grand-daughters gathered together in the evening for a chat and a song, and duels were fought between old lovers across the room.

Sweet Lily, going eighty, and nifty at dominoes (till they were banned after a lunchtime brawl in the back-room) had an impressive high-pitched voice with much-admired quivering glissandos. Her nightly performances came to a sudden end one icy morning as she slipped off the pavement and broke an ankle.

We got her a clapped-out wheelchair from Miller's Auction Rooms, and began to wheel her to the pub of a night time. She enjoyed the rides so much her friends started hinting that she'll never walk again. After six weeks I gave up with the wheeling and she got up. She never forgot or forgave.

I made – and lost – younger friends too. A teenage couple, newly married and much in love, asked for a photograph off me as they left the street to join the Army. As a special token she had dyed her lovely long hair blonde to look like me, and they sang for me their last night in the pub. I never saw them again, except in his mother's photographs.

Demolition

From 1972 onwards the demolition really got underway. You would see 'e/off' (for 'electricity off') daubed on doors, which would occasionally become 'f/off'! Door after door received this stamp of death.

Bricked up, deaf and dumb façades of empty streets invited fleeting dark thoughts: I wondered if they all got out! The demolition was catching up with Byker. The count-down on streets and houses and friends began; the melancholia set in.

The wash-house closed down, and for many months after the merry celebrations and dancing and singing, the women who toiled and gossiped and laughed together in the steam and the noise sat lost and lonely in the coin-operated launderette beyond the main street, complaining about the price and the inefficiency of the machines.

Where Did They Go?

The pork butcher moved to North Shields to start a new business; the cobbler retired and left for Canada to join his daughter. Mrs Potter, born, wed and widowed in a street as old as herself, kindly closed her door on the man who came to sell her a wonderful future elsewhere. 'Thank you, hinny, but I belong

Conyers Road and Parker Street come tumbling down around resistant corner-shops, 1970. The No. 12 bus runs along a homeless Brinkburn Road. Clive Terrace remains in the background.

Conyers Road and Albion Row present grim stubs of what used to be, as the demolition of old Byker proceeds apace in 1969. In the City behind, St James's Park today stands at the level of the crane top!

116

here.' Mr and Mrs McCartney sat amongst their packed-up boxes in an empty house for a year and a half waiting to be moved. 'We'll be siting here till the day we die, hinny…' The conversation in the streets skated around who's going, gone, where and when. Who died only a week after moving. Who never saw a new house at all. They used to tell me about everything and sometimes it was hard to know where the truth ended. These are stories I was told and wrote down but regrettably without getting a name.

These pieces are extracts from Sirkka's tapes for which she was unable to get a name.

Big Families

Families were big in our day; there were ten of us, we were like bloody rats. Me mother had twins that died, well that makes twelve. For all our da had a cobbler's shop, none of us had a pair of shoes when we was kids.

New Shoes

'One day me father telt us to gan to Shields Road for twopenn'orth of bacon pieces. It was freezing cold; eight o'clock in the morning and I was waiting outside the shop, for the shop to open at eight-thirty; I had to go to school for nine. I was stannin' on me hands what with the cold - no shoes you see? A gentleman came by and he says: 'Got no shoes, sonny?' I says 'No.' He says: 'Come with me.' He took us across the road to a shoe shop and bought us a pair of shoes. He tries them on us in the shop; I had no stockings. 'Ooh,' I says, 'they are smashing.' I was frightened in case he took them off us,

The world-weary back lanes of Kendal Street become overgrown as the people move out, 1972.

you see? So there's me with the bacon and the shoe box, and me dad says: 'Where did you get those?' I says: 'A gentleman bought them for us on Shields Road!' Proud as punch were I. Well, they were that tight I couldn't get them off. Me dad pulled them off me and gave them to a younger brother.

Infant Mortality

Me aunt Harriet Taylor had twenty-two children and a lodger. She lived above Shepherds rag shop down Byker Bank, and she only had the one big room. Alive with rats it were, and they all had to sleep and live in it.

There was one day she was lying in bed having this bairn, and there's two lying in coffins waiting to be carried out. She used to get them to a certain age, and then they would die. Well, she run out of names, there was eventually three called Harry. She was the kindest of women. She had no money 'cause her man used to drink a lot and wouldn't tip up. But every Sunday you went out she would have a ha'penny lined on the mantelpiece for you.

Passing Comments

Feedback from Byker is no longer simply the concern of Newcastle. The ideas generated here will be turning up in all kinds of places around the world...

Diana Rowntree

Lose the people and it just won't be Byker any more.

Ralph Erskine (Byker Wall architect)

The rather sober apparel adopted by widowed older women is seen here on a hot August day in 1900. She is thought to be crossing the NER line near Dalton Street.

They're canny folk around here.

Anon., Mason Street

It's the houses that want changing – not the people.

Anon.

Sirkka came away from her short interlude in Byker speaking Finnish with a Geordie accent and never quite understanding how her sojourn in this strange corner of Newcastle was to forever change her life. Not only did her experience here shape her thinking towards her later work involving people but her name was destined to be forever inextricably linked

The entire working staff of Lee, Holme & Co. Third from right in the back row is Mrs Bromley (née Lord). The contributor of the picture was reliably informed that no-one could remove the skin of a rabbit in one movement as she could. She would make the pelts into slippers for relatives. (Courtesy of the Byker Phoenix).

with the Byker community in a way that even the most extrovert pub singer will never be. These are her final thoughts:

When my house finally came down with a clean sweep from the swinging ball, I stood and watched, gulping, at a distance. From that moment I began to miss my downstairs neighbour who sent the incredible Hulk [her husband] to raise hell about my antique Hoover interfering with her telly; who patiently stood on her doorstep clocking in and out my friends; who directed visitors to my house saying: It's the only dirty step in the street, you can't miss it.'

The Start of the New Byker

In the new Byker they built an orange grove in the name of Councillor Theresa Russell, 'for all the hard work she had done in the Byker District'.

The first rents were £4.55 a week for rent, water and central heating. It was 'fair', say most residents. Families were first moved into 'test' homes. They were asked to complain about anything and everything that they felt could be improved upon. The first resident into the final homes, on 29 July 1971, was seventy-year-old Jim Gilbert of Kendal Street. Jim was a retired pottery foreman.

The corner shop wasn't a shop so much as

A 1970 view through the stubs that were Parker Street and Clifford Street. Workers from Lowrie's egg factory make their way home.

Like a phoenix, the new Byker grows, 1973.

a club where they sold things. It sometimes took three hours to buy a packet of fags. I see Byker as many corner-shops, pubs and, yes, the bath-house. Places of social significance.

James Doolan

Places Long Gone

Dents Hole was a part of Byker and was a pirate anchorage and small village in its own right up to about 1825 when the Tyne Improvement Commissioners began reprofiling the river into its modern shape. What was Dents Hole is now the allotments adjoining the river.

Elders Walker Yard in the Ouseburn employed a lot of Byker people. It was situated near the Loraine Arms. The Ouseburn area was a very smelly place prior to the clean up and new culvert construction operations, begun in 1906/07.

Ernie Neil

Hadrian's Wall

The Janet Street development contract was given to Leeds Builders for £1.6 million and was called the Janet Croft development. This was without doubt the poorest work of the entire scheme. There were numerous strikes and disputes and 'down-tools' etc. They were officially declared bankrupt in about May 1979 and the builders abandoned the site. It remained in this state – unfinished – until 1984. It took another £2 million to re-energize the project. The half-finished mess was bulldozed in June 1984 and the final thirty-eight dwellings were completed in 1995 – the final piece of this huge jig-saw that had been born in 1962 within the old ivory towers of a Dan Smith City Hall. A mere thirty-three years!

They're still digging up bits of old Byker here in 2000! In October, whilst digging around outside the Byker 'wet and wild' Swimming Baths they finally managed to find the 'missing link.' This was the find that had mystified archaeologists over the years, until then, that is. What they found was the missing piece to confirm without doubt that the course of Hadrian's Wall went through this part of Byker. What they therefore found was the first Byker Wall – only about fifty yards from the 1970 'wall'. I hope they open it up as the 'Roman Byker Wall'. It'll be another attraction for Byker's tourist economy!

The 'Avondale' sector of the Byker Wall was planned to be the last neighbourhood to be rebuilt to Erskine's plans. It was eventually built in 1980/81 and consisted of 134 houses and flats, and cost about £2.6 million.

Ken Groundwater

Byker's Limits

Byker begins where the Tyne-Tees TV studios stop lording it over the Quayside and it goes on until, all of a sudden, it turns into Heaton. It turns into Heaton just as the frog turns into the fairy prince. Byker, fighting for air, then suddenly lah-di-dah Heaton heaven and no need to fight anymore!

Keith Armstrong

Thirties Modernization

I was born in one of the houses between the two Byker Bridges (as there was then) and eventually lived in three of them. I married a Byker lad and we set up house in one in 1942. I couldn't tell you about all the characters down the 'Burn' – there was so many! The shop nearby was known for its 'treacle taffy'. I remember a film being made thereabouts called *On the Night of the Fire* including Ralph Richardson (later

In 1973, problems with contractors saw stages of the Wall work delayed.

The Byker Wall closes across the top of old Raby Street whilst life goes on, 1973.

Sir), and I remember our mothers walking about as extras. My mother got 5s for the use of her pinny which she had to get scruffy for them. It was down the 'Burn' that I first saw modernization, thirties style – when they knocked two houses together through a wall and made a passage into the back of one house and put in water, sink and a small bench and that was your living room. The other house was your bedroom. Now we were posh. We had a front door and a back door but we still had to go about 50 yards to the toilet in what we called the top yard.

Mona Milor

Old Byker Bank

Reproduced by permission of Jack Routledge.

They're pulling down old Byker Bank,
Down come those old streets rank on rank.
Oh, fare you well old Raby Street,
You leave behind you memories so sweet.

When we were kids we used to roam
All over Byker, miles from home;
Down to the Burn and the old Quayside
To watch the ships along the river tide.

And now their end those hooses meet
from Union Road to Dalton Street;
From Shepherds' Yard to Albion Row
The wreckers pull the ropes and doon they go.

The wash house standing in the rain,
The smell of washing through a broken pane,
The tram cars thundered as they swayed along,
The trolley buses sang their silent song.

Down Granny's Park we used to play
A football match that'd last all day.
Then to the Playgie just to be seen
The parkie chased us off the bowling green.

We used to run up and doon the lanes,
From top to bottom and back again;
But now those back lanes they are no more –
You can't play football on the fourteenth floor.

And now old Byker has been pulled down,
They're building us a brand new town.
We hope the planners can understand
You can't build people out of bricks and sand.

Now we live in super flats,
We can't keep pigeons, dogs or cats;
To pay the rent is awful hard
But from the top you can see the Naval Yard.

A *war-damaged part of Grafton Street undergoes clearance, 29 January 1958. The view includes Woolworth's and Beaven's Shields Road stores. (NCL)*

Byker's History

Before the above, no-one had ever written a song about Byker. If they had it is possible that Geordies who have never been there would have been proud to acknowledge it as part of their great city of Newcastle. But, alas, the proud people of Byker remain unknown to the outside world and yet their claim to fame is as great as those that live in other parts of the city. There was a time, long ago, when it was far removed from the city and used to have a customs barrier for wool between the town and Byker village. In 1346 one of the customs men was himself convicted of smuggling wool across the Tyne from Gateshead to Byker, to avoid duty. Industry began in Byker as long ago as 1619 with the appearance of the glass industry at Glasshouse Bridge. By 1825 there were the two glasshouses, five potteries, three wind flourmills, one steam flourmill, two mills for grinding flint, one lead factory. One flax mill, one chemical works, two copper works, one tannery, one skinnery and a glue factory had swept a lot of farming Byker away forever. Until 1835 Byker was part of Northumberland but after this time the City wanted some of its wealth.

Joan Elliot

Waiting for Rehousing: 1970s

Isabella is from one of only seven families left in Grace Street and has been awaiting rehousing for four years.

We have had five different moving dates. My nerves are at breaking point and I hardly dare to leave the house in case vandals break in, thinking its derelict. See the gaps around here, ours is the last few houses standing with these huge gaps between. We have been offered an old house in Benton but have decided to wait for one of the new flats so we can stay in Byker. It's got to such a stage now where I can't invite anyone back because I'm so ashamed of the state of the house. Many's the time I have passed friends on Shields Road but I don't ask them home any more.

Isabella Morgan

Noisy Pigeons

Since the house next door is half-demolished the pigeons have moved in and we cannot get any sleep for the noise they make in the rafters above us. I can't understand why the entire street wasn't cleared at once. We have been offered a house outside Byker, but we want a new place after all these years waiting, anyway Byker is our home. We were first told we would be rehoused last September, then it was February this year. I'll believe it when I see it. The vandals are never away. We have been half packed, ready to go, for the last three years. I can't stand this for another three years.

James Graham

Culvert construction work on the Ouseburn under way, c. 1907. The ironic comment by the photographer may refer to the rich colour of the old tip. (NCL)

125

Lower Ouseburn

The majority of the Lower Ouseburn area comes under the All Saints Ward, whilst the upper area of the vale was split between the Byker and Heaton Wards. It is steeped in history and has its own magazine Ouseburn Heritage, *produced by Mike Greatbatch (who has done so much to draw interesting history out of nothing). Mike has lived and breathed this area for a long time and had these things to say:*

I've spent a lot of time in this area and the things that excite me about it are the simple things you come across when out walking these streets about Ouseburn. You can see St Silas' parish church foundation stone was laid down by Miss Maling of the local Maling pottery family on 26 November 1885 and stands today as the main Byker area parish church, having taken over the responsibilities when St Michael's on Byker Hill closed two years ago. Beyond the church you pass the end of Albion Row and Quality Row – two vintage early Byker constructions – and if you keep going down Byker Bank you come out at Ford Street with its connotations with the now gone huge pottery works which was nearby. Mary Ford married Charles Maling in 1857 and he was able to make good use of her dowry wealth to expand his pottery empire into this area, to capitalize upon the extensive clay deposits around. A large grassy area comes into view on your left hand side along Ford Street and this is one of the most historic sites in Byker. It is the first burial ground for the district and shows up on maps as the Ballast Hills Burial Ground. An examination of those gravestones still readable reveals victims of several plagues in the 1700s and hence its local name 'The Plaguey Fields'. Large numbers were deposited during 1831-32, 1848-49 and 1853 [during cholera epidemics] and will still be enveloped at a minimum of six feet down in quick-lime after their hasty funerals (within twelve hours of death). Alongside is the Ouseburn Board School which was built in 1853 and closed in 1960. Talking to others, I found that it is rumoured that a headmaster hanged himself on the Plaguey Field behind the school; also that a female teacher hanged herself inside the school – was teaching then that stressful? The school is now a Grade II listed building and opened as a Business Development Centre in 1993. It is of a curious architectural design – just look at those Dutch-looking gables, the dark red brickwork and, to cap it all, it has an eastern-looking pagoda-style turrets adding to the architectural curiosity of Byker and its recent wall design.

Nearby more streets tell their past history via their names: Foundry Lane, Lime Street and Glasshouse Bridge, not perhaps too romantic but they have this 'no frills' Byker functionality that reflects the area's lack of pretensions.

Mike Greatbatch

Ouseburn

Cleaning-up operations began in 1972/73 and a reclamation scheme to tidy up this area began. Cosmetic work done to cover parts of the exposed Ouse stream. Then the work started on the Metro Bridge which was built over the top of the site between 1976 and '79 and was officially

The reduction in freight carried to the shipyards by rail saw St Peter's station decline to a shed as a signal box and little else by 1972.

North Shields Railway. It eventually became part of the East Coast main line to Scotland but had to have another viaduct built alongside the first to make a four-track section over the top. The original construction was rebuilt in iron in 1867 and the new extra viaduct alongside came in 1887 to complete the bridge as we see it today.

Under the Ouseburn Viaduct, off Stepney Bank, and covering an area of contaminated land which was once a lead works, today is the Byker City Farm. It began life in 1976 and copied an earlier

At the western edge, the Ouseburn Viaduct forms a tangible boundary between Byker and the City lights. Demolition is going on in South View as a diesel train heads towards Newcastle. 1979.

opened on 11 November 1982 as part of the St James-Tynemouth section opening of the Metro System when Byker got its second station to have this name. The first was the Byker station near Riverside Junction and access was from Roger Street off Shields Road. The line ran alongside Albion Row and Dalton Street for a good way and had sidings that ran into the Ford Pottery of Malings. They used to take some traffic out of there up till the thirties but didn't do much after the war.

Construction of the Viaduct began in 1837 and was opened in May 1839 to enable the opening of the Newcastle and

The white-fronted Chillingham Hotel can be seen to the right of the train front at Heaton Junction in this 1983 view. The then new Metro system is at the extreme left and prepares to dive under Shields Road before arriving at the second Byker station.

'city-farm' idea that was successful at Kentish Town. It survived the early years via MSC schemes but when these stopped in 1980, it seemed as if the farm might go under. It didn't, and became a registered charity and has gone from strength to strength. The kids around the area all go through stages of visiting night after night straight from school and helping muck out etc. It has brought them experiences that would otherwise be denied inner-city dwellers and has been a brilliant educational idea. Byker people love their farm.

Ken Groundwater